THE
ROSE MANUAL

BOOKS IN THE
OLD ROSES SERIES

THE ROSE GARDEN
by William Paul

THE ROSE MANUAL
by Robert Buist

THE BOOK OF ROSES
or,
THE ROSE FANCIER'S MANUAL
by Catherine Frances Gore

HISTORY OF THE ROSE
by Roy E. Shepherd

OLD ROSES
by Ethelyn Emery Keays

OLD GARDEN ROSES
by Edward A. Bunyard

THE
ROSE MANUAL

Robert Buist

New Foreword by
Edith C. Shurr

EARL M. COLEMAN, Publisher
New York   1978

Library of Congress Cataloging in Publication Data

Buist, Robert, 1805–1880.
  The rose manual.

  (Old roses series)
  Reprint of the 1844 ed. published by the author in
Philadelphia.
  1. Roses—Varieties. I. Title. II. Series.
SB411.B92 1978   635.9′33′372   78-9704
ISBN 0-930576-10-1

ISBN 0-930476-10-1

This Earl M. Coleman edition of
THE ROSE MANUAL
is a faithful facsimile reproduction
of the first edition published
in Philadelphia in 1844.
It includes a new Foreword
prepared for this edition.

©1978 by Earl M. Coleman, Publisher
875 Avenue of the Americas
New York, NY 10001

FOREWORD TO THE 1978 EDITION

Robert Buist was a happy man. Born in Scotland in 1802, he enjoyed a lifetime of enthusiastic and ever-expanding interest and practice of floriculture, with vocation and avocation completely merged to provide rewards in personal pleasure and commercial success.

He was entirely his own man; well acquainted with the prominent rose growers of the U.S., Great Britain, Holland, Germany and France, he appreciated their accomplishments but never in any particular copied or imitated their writings. A review of his *Rose Manual* in the "London's Gardener's Magazine" said, "This differs from most of the American works on gardening, in being an original composition from beginning to end... There is no American work that we know of, at all, to be compared with it in point of usefulness."

As a very young lad in Scotland, Robert Buist became interested in floriculture and later became manager of the famous Edinburgh Gardens. In 1828 he came to Philadelphia, where he lived and worked happily and successfully. He died in 1880. His son, Robert Jr., who had grown up working with his father, was to carry on the family business.

What started out as Robert Buist's Seed Store soon had to be enlarged to include general gardening supplies, potted plants, shrubs and small fruits, rose bushes and a florist business. By 1837 it had outgrown its original location. In that year Mr. Buist moved to larger quarters on 12th Street, below Lombard. The firm had been a partnership, Hibbert & Buist, terminated by the sudden death of Mr. Hibbert, but Buist retained the same name until the 1837 move. Needing ever more space, he moved again to Market Street in 1857. The final move, in 1870, was to 67th Street near Darby Road. The Buist farm, Bonaffon, was located in the section of Philadelphia through which Buist Avenue now runs.

Robert Buist was a master gardener, a talented teacher, and a very proficient writer. In writing, as in speaking, there is no substitute for sound knowledge of the subject. That knowledge he had, along with enthusiastic love and joy in gardening and in sharing his skill by helping others. Two of his books were *The American Florist Guide* and *Buist's (Robert) Family Kitchen Gardener*, published by C. M. Caxton, Barker & Company, in New York. His fine *American Flower Garden Directory*, published in 1832, was so successful that it went through six editions.

Buist became acquainted with the prominent American rose growers and visted Great Britain and the Continent every year or two in order to keep informed about their introductions and propagating practices. He imported the roses which seemed best to him, buying his stock mostly from Mr. Hardy of the Luxembourg Gardens in Paris.

Imagine Buist's delight when, in 1832, he met the famous *Madame Hardy*, one of the outstanding roses of all time, still widely grown and shown, still greatly loved by any grower of old garden roses and on many a list of favorites. He wrote, *"Globe Hip, White Globe,* or *Boule de Neige* of the French, is an English Rose raised from seeds of the common white, a very pure white, fully double and of globular form. A few years ago it was considered 'not to be surpassed', but that prediction, like many others, has fallen to the ground, and now *Madame Hardy* is triumphant, being larger, fully as pure, more double, and an abundant bloomer; the foliage and wood are also stronger. The French describe it as 'large, very double pure white, and of cup or bowl form'". *Madame Hardy* was an immediate success, written about by Rose writers in glowing terms, except for the surprising prejudice of Dean Hole, who described the Madame as "showing the green eye of jealousy" in displaying the green pip in the bloom which is generally admired, and is pointed out as final proof in identification. Buist happily carried the lovely Madame home to Philadelphia with him and introduced it there classed as an Alba, though he wrote that it "belongs perhaps more properly to the Damask or Gallica" class, which is its present classification, as Damask.

In 1839 Buist, visiting another of his suppliers, J. P. Vibert, of Lonjeameaux, near Paris, found there the fine *Aimée Vibert* which he brought back home and introduced. He explained that his "enthusiasm can be easily understood by those who, like myself, have been so fortunate as to see the two *'Aimée Viberts'*—the rose and the young girl—both in their full bloom, and both as lovely as their sweet name". He further reported that "*Aimée Vibert,* or *Nevia,* is a beautiful pure white, perfect in form, a profuse bloomer, but though quite hardy does not grow freely for us; however, when budded on a strong stock it makes a

4

magnificent standard, and blooms with a profusion not surpassed by any".

Another best seller for the Buist Nursery was *River's George the Fourth* which he admired and brought back from a visit to Thomas Rivers & Son, in England. It is unfortunately one of the fine old roses now almost nonexistent in the U.S., very rare and with no source for buying it.

It is in fact tragic and discouraging that so many of the roses listed have disappeared in the century since Robert Buist's death; a few undoubtedly remain, unrecognized and unsung unless they are found by the treasure hunters among Old Rose addicts. It is one of the principles of the recently formed Heritage Roses Group to provide budwood of rare varieties in hopes that the sharing will lead to bringing them back into production and general appreciation.

One difficulty in equating the Buist Rose names and classifications with modern terms can be accounted for in the many changes in nomenclature that continue to the present. He brought with him to America the British fondness for understatement but when he became enthusiastic about the Noisette Roses, he somewhat exaggerated their importance by assigning many roses he propagated or imported for sale to his broad category as Noisettes. He was apt to call all white roses "Albas", but he was not willing to join in the custom of calling some roses "Evergreen" or "Ever-blooming" when they were not. He described his roses exactly as he saw them and watched them grow and bloom in his own fields. He was sharply critical of the underhanded business practices of some rose growers, saying that "it is truly a disgrace to any vendor or amateur to change the name of any rose knowingly, merely to prevent his brethren in the trade from reaping at once any benefit by procuring the article from its original source. . . American growers are not so directly criminal in this respect, but they are frequently led into error by purchasing from some French Importers, who, in many instances, have plants to suit any name or colour. We are also occasionally caught by our English rose-growers, who in visiting France, pick up the surplus stock of any new and choice rose, take it home, advertise boldly under a new name, and sell it at a golden price." In another chapter he remarked that "There are more names than there are roses." Does that sound familiar to you? There are many old roses known under two or three names, sometimes by the use of endearing nicknames, or from different localities, but too often because of the chicanery described by

6

Robert Buist. He was trapped himself once when he sold a highly recommended "new rose" for the thumping price of $5.00, only to learn, to his great chagrin, that it was an old one under a new name. He had luckily sold only three and was able to reclaim those and make restitution to his neighbors at once. We have all been sold mis-labelled roses, by chance or by deliberate intent. In a few cases a famous rose has masqueraded for years under an assumed name, though not intentionally; an error almost impossible to correct.

In addition to the sometimes puzzling classifications used by Buist, his description of types takes some getting used to: "dwarf", "standard", "stocks", "climbers" and "climbing hybrids", for instance. We don't think of a rose bush from two to three feet tall as being "dwarf". What he called "standards" were bud-grafted plants on understock from one to six feet high— "trees". On pruning, he was explicit, instructing not only the proper time of year for pruning but also how many bud-eyes to leave on the plant.

It must be remembered that Buist wrote his *Rose Manual* for his customers in the United States. He himself was much more at home in Great Britain, Paris and the rose-growing areas in France, Germany and even

Holland than in American localities any distance from Philadelphia. He knew his San Francisc﹚ publishers only by correspondence and so far as we know he never traveled beyond the eastern and nearby southern states.

Robert Buist was ahead of his time, fearlessly championing the actual growing of Roses by females. In all the history of the rose, only a few feminine names appear, and those never relating to any actual work performed. Collecting and growing roses was a man's game until at least the early 1800's. The men of action—explorers, traders, the Crusaders, early botanists and travelers—found and brought back rose specimens from far places, carrying them around the known world.

The Empress Josephine, who had a famous rose collection in her gardens near Paris, gave the impetus to rose-growing which actually began the programs of planned hybridizing. She used her wealth and power to try to accumulate all the known roses and was even able to transcend the difficulties of exchanging roses with nations that were at war. She commissioned the famous and capable Pierre-Joseph Redouté to paint her roses and the fine rosarian, C. A. Thory, with writing the descriptions. She made rose growing fashionable for all of Europe and undoubtedly saved for us many roses of historical importance which would otherwise have been lost. But there is no evidence that she actually grew the roses herself.

Buist built up a business of selling roses to his neighborhood ladies, whom he called his Patronesses. It was for them that he wrote his *Rose Manual*, which was planned and written in minute detail as a complete handbook for the true novice. He left out nothing. In fact his instructions were sometimes a bit monotonous, repeated for emphasis and intended to explain clearly what to do to raise roses. His message was that anyone could plan a garden, ready the soil, plant the roses, take care of them properly, and enjoy success. It is no wonder that his Ladies responded enthusiastically, as he took them from the first planning and soil preparation to every known method of propagation.

The only illustrations in the *Rose Manual* are the clear steel engravings, one depicting the method of making a tree rose and the others explaining methods of grafting. The chapter on Diseases and Insects could well be copied by our modern ecologists. Buist never saw a Japanese beetle, red spider-mite, or a tent caterpillar, but he was able to cope with mildew, green fly, die-back, winter

9

damage and "general malaise" by recommending proper locations, sensible enrichment, adequate watering, proper pruning and liberal dousing with soapy water. He explained the use of each rose, its ideal location, and which were best for each purpose, even pointing out which should be grafted and which grew better on their own roots. He taught the Ladies exactly how to hybridize roses, though as far as I know none ever ventured to try it. Indeed, there are too few women in that field even today.

Buist gave helpful advice and encouragement to Miss Louisa Johnson and, when her book was published, mentioned it kindly in his *American Flower Garden Directory*. Her title for this rather daring work expressed his philosophy and obviously hers: "*Every Lady Her Own Flower Gardener*, addressed to the Industrious and Economical ONLY."

I first read Robert Buist's *Rose Manual* some twelve or thirteen years ago and acquired *The American Flower Garden Directory* several years later. Roses have always been an important part of my life and I was then trying to collect old garden roses of every class, especially those I first knew as a toddler, grown by my parents and grandparents. My grandparents bought roses from Robert Buist and later from Robert Jr., ordering from the vast distance of their first home in Ohio and then from the even more distant "western land" when they moved to a farm in southern Iowa soon after the Civil War. I suspect that the jolly marbled Gallicas, on their own roots, which were moved down to our home in Missouri after Grandpa's death when Grandma Mac sold the farm, were supplied by Buist Nursery. They were moved about 1908 or 1909. Grandma remained an active rosarian in her own home for many years, and then while living with us. She was always spry and enjoyed the roses to the end of her 83 years, in 1923. She was also a teacher, ever instructing and admonishing, so that when I first read the *Rose Manual* and found so much that was familiar, I thought how interesting it was that this writer agreed with all the rose lore I had learned from Grandma Mac, my mother, and from my own experience. I have always believed in the sensible "home remedies" because I admire the wonderful abilities of Nature to cope with growing things. I have advocated growing roses on their own roots, I approve of sloshing roses with soapy water and so on, but I have been slow in realizing that—by inheritance—I am actually one of Mr. Buist's Ladies. Grandma was one, Mother learned his ways from her, and I grew up being instructed by both of them. Thank you, Mr. Buist.

Edith Campbell Schurr
Edmonds, Washington
February, 1978

THE

ROSE MANUAL;

CONTAINING

ACCURATE DESCRIPTIONS OF ALL THE FINEST VARIETIES

OF

ROSES,

PROPERLY CLASSED IN THEIR RESPECTIVE FAMILIES,
THEIR CHARACTER AND MODE OF CULTURE,

WITH

DIRECTIONS FOR THEIR PROPAGATION,

AND THE DESTRUCTION OF INSECTS.

WITH ENGRAVINGS.

———————

BY ROBERT BUIST,

NURSERYMAN AND FLORIST.

———————

PHILADELPHIA.

FOR THE AUTHOR AND MESSRS. CAREY AND HART.

1844.

INTRODUCTION.

Custom has made it the privilege of authors to set forth the merit and purport of their productions in some preliminary remarks. Of this privilege I gladly avail myself, to disclaim at once all pretensions to the art of composition.

These pages owe their existence merely to the repeated demands of numerous friends and customers, for a work on Roses, simple in its arrangement, and clear in its directions. I have endeavoured to gratify their wishes, and have now only to hope that their satisfaction may bear some proportion to the pleasure I have found in the task.

This volume contains the result of twenty years' experience on the subject of which it treats, fifteen of which have been as a nurseryman cultivating the largest collection in the country. I do not wish to be understood, however, as arrogating to myself any greater share of knowledge in rose culture than can be acquired by all practical men. But it is not to these that I address myself. My humble aim has been to present to the unexperienced lovers of the ROSE, a guide to enable them to select, cultivate, and propagate their favourite flower. The undertaking has occupied the greater part of my leisure hours for the past two years, during which period, observations made among the numerous collections of nurserymen and amateurs in this vicinity, induced me frequently to alter descriptions I had already written, colours varying to so great an extent in different soils and seasons.

I have endeavoured to bring all my descriptions to the standard of a mere admiring amateur; admitting that many roses resemble each other in colour and form, while to a practised eye they may appear very distinct in growth and other characters.

The first season after planting, roses do not, in general, flower in all the perfection to which they can be brought after one or two years growth, taking that time to become thoroughly established. A few of the new kinds have bloomed but once; a very accurate description of such can scarcely be expected; and in some instances it may hereafter appear that I have not done full justice to their

real merit. Amateurs have hitherto found great
difficulty in selecting from the catalogues of nurserymen. This treatise, we hope, may be found of
service in assisting them to form their collections;
and the index of names, referring, as it does, to the
character of every rose mentioned in the work,
will, we think, prove especially useful.

Incorrectness in the name of plants has long
been a stigma on commercial gardening; none can
pretend to be quite immaculate in this matter,
but all may become still more careful in avoiding
these inaccuracies. Every nurseryman is now
aware of the great responsibility resting upon him
in correct nomenclature, and no honest man will
condescend to contribute in spreading the practice
of attaching a false name. On this point we think
Philadelphia nurserymen are as free from reproach
as any in the Union, and I may be permitted to
add, that in rose culture they are adepts, living, as
they do, as it were in a very *hotbed of roses*, fos-
tered by the judicious management of the Horticultural Society, and encouraged by the patronage
of the lovers of flowers, who, amongst us, are
almost as numerous as the dwellings of our city
and county. It would be ungrateful not to add

my sincere acknowledgments to all those to whom I am indebted for valuable information, and in an especial manner to a lady amateur, whose valuable services have frequently brightened our ideas. And finally, let me be allowed to place this humble offering under the patronage of the LADIES, trusting that their love of the subject will induce them to look over all deficiencies in the manner of treating it, and hoping that the views and experience of a practical man, honestly given, and in a style aiming at nothing but perspicuity, may be of some use to them. While it has been my object to produce a manual adapted to the wants of every rose fancier, I have been especially anxious to make the task of selection an easier one to my fair patronesses, and if I succeed in assisting any of them in the choice or culture of a single rose I shall be satisfied;—or should I be the means of inducing some to enter the flowery paths of horticulture, where healthful employment and innocent pleasures wait to greet them, my highest ambition will be attained.

PHILADELPHIA, *March*, 1844.

CONTENTS.

~~~~~~~~~~

ROSES THAT BLOOM IN JUNE.

ROSA ALPINA.

THE BOURSAULT ROSE.

THIS tribe takes its name from the late Mons. Boursault, a distinguished French amateur horticulturist. They are the hardiest of the climbing roses—easily known by their long flexible shoots, of a reddish-purple colour, and withstanding with impunity the severest of our winters, flowering profusely early in the season; they may well be termed the harbingers of the rosary. They are well adapted for covering arbours or concealing outbuildings, walls, or any other disagreeable objects. They are also frequently cultivated for stocks, whereon to bud other roses of more rare character, which purpose they will answer very well; though a plant thus formed renders its durability uncertain, being very liable to *sucker*, or throw out shoots from the ground, thereby taking away nourishment from the part of the plant which

2

most requires it; of course, all suckers or shoots below the bud or graft must be displaced. It was introduced in 1829–30. The following sorts are most worthy of notice:

Amadis or *Elegans* are the same; of rapid growth, makes a most magnificent pyramid of rich purple crimson; the flowers are produced in clusters, are perfectly double, and of considerable duration. *White Boursault*, Blush, Bengal Florida, Rose de Lisle, the same rose, known under all these, and even some other names; the flowers are very large, of a blush colour, with a deep pink centre, pendulous, and very showy, but occasionally do not open well. *Gracilis*, is of slender growth, with bright pink flowers, not fully double, but very profuse. *Inermis*, has large bright pink flowers, in great profusion; grows rapidly, and is rendered the more desirable by having a little fragrance, of which, with this exception, this group are entirely destitute. *Purpurea*, purple crimson flowers, little more than half double; it is the most common of the tribe, and has been extensively cultivated and sold under the name of Purple Noisette, *Maheka*, *Michigan* &c., and is cultivated and sold from the flat boats on the Ohio and Mississippi rivers under all these and several other names; compared with the preceding sorts, it is not worth culture. *Red* or *Pink* is the oldest variety with flowers only semidouble; the colour is pretty, and its profusion, at a distance, makes up for deficiency of petals. The species Rosa Alpina is a native of the Alps, where its scrubby habit has little affinity to the rampant growers now described. They should have, wherever planted, plenty of space allotted for them; for after being one or two years established, they will make shoots ten to twelve feet long. In pruning, the oldest wood should be cut out, merely to keep the branches from being too crowded: the flowers are produced from the wood of the preceding year. They will grow freely in any soil or situation, and will bear with impunity the severest winters of the northern states.

ROSA SEMPERVIRENS.

THE EVERGREEN ROSE.

THIS rose and its varieties, although very popular in France and England, lose much of the character implied by the name when cultivated in this part of the United States, where they become deciduous, losing their foliage on the approach of severe frost. But in the more favoured southern

climes, they retain it during winter, and there grow
and bloom in profuse wreaths or garlands, making
them objects of great attraction in their season.
They are in colour generally pale, making a de-
cided contrast with the Boursault family. They
grow rapidly, and are well adapted for arches,
grottos, rockwork, pillars, or trellises. The foliage
is of a peculiarly bright shining green. *Adelaide
d'Orleans* has flowers of a pale rosy blush, very
double and perfectly formed, in large clusters,
valuable for blooming later than any of what are
termed June Roses. *Donna Maria*, and Princess
Maria, appear to be the same, or so nearly alike, that
a distinction cannot be even faintly drawn. Flowers
nearly white. *Felicite Perpetuelle* has been recognized under many names in Europe, but it is
believed to be *pure* here : it is a very perfect rose,
beautifully cupped, of a creamy-white colour, and
when well grown makes a magnificent pyramid.
Myrianthes is of the most regular form, being
very double, and imbricated to the centre ; a plant
covered with its delicate rosy coloured flowers is a
charming object. It has been sold (as its name
imports) as a Noisette, *blooming all the season*, a
character which it never merited, never had, and
never will have. *Sempervirens Pleno*, a pure
white, is our oldest variety, perfectly double, and
a very desirable rose ; it is the parent of Noisette

Aimée Vibert, an association which will long preserve it from oblivion. *Triomphe de Bollwiller*, is
a superb blush-white rose, very large, very double,
in great clusters, and agreeably fragrant; in the
south it is surprisingly fine, but with us it is rather
tender.   When this rose first made its appearance
in France, it *came out* as the most beautiful of the
"Teas;" after its more general cultivation it was
placed among the Noisettes; it now falls back to
those sorts that only bloom once, where it is now
distinguished under the name of *Sempervirens odorata*.   After fourteen years travel through the
French catalogue it is now *set down* where it
should have been placed at first, a situation given
to it by me four years ago.   There are several other
varieties of Rosa Sempervirens, but none of sufficient interest or distinction from the above to claim
any detailed notice.   In the southern states, this
family, associated with *Rosa Laevigata* or *Georgia
Evergreen Rose*, would make a very splendid group
for covering fences, embankments, or any other object where a continual foliage was desirable; they
require very little pruning, and would soon cover a
large space.   They could be propagated by layering to any extent; any good soil will suit their
growth.   They could also be used for covering the
naked stems of trees with great advantage, in an
ornamental point of view; if used for such a pur-

pose they will require a portion of manure dug
into the ground about their roots every winter. In
pruning the wood of several years old should be
cut out, only laying in the young shoots their full
length; these shoots can be turned and twisted in
any direction; although it is decidedly best to lay
them in straight and equal.

ROSA BANKSIANA.

THE LADY BANKS ROSE.

WHEN this rose-first made its appearance in the
time of Sir Joseph Banks, it was hailed with the
greatest rapture by every lover of the tribe, and it
was instantly complimented with the name of his
lady. It is the states south of this where it must
be seen to be pronounced the most graceful, luxuriant, and beautiful of roses; there it is a perfect
evergreen, covering the ends, fronts, and, in some
instances, the entire dwellings of many of the
inhabitants, who name it the "*Evergreen Multiflora.*" To us, the beauty of the plant is nearly
lost, being too tender for planting in the garden,
and when grown in the greenhouse, its beauty and
luxuriance almost disappear. This thornless rose

is so perfectly double that it rarely produces seed.
Although many European growers recognize and
sell several varieties of Banksia Roses, yet there
are only two, in our opinion, that deserve attention; the others are hybrids, mere misnomers. One
catalogue offers twenty-one varieties, all beautifully
named, our goodly city being complimented by
Philadelphica having a place in the list. The
flowers are produced on the small twigy branches,
hence it is important to divest the plants of any long
rampant growth, that it may set forth, unless it is
required to lay in to fill up any vacancy. The
White Banksian Rose has flowers little more than
half an inch in diameter, which are of the purest
white, with a delicate pink centre of a very delightful violet perfume, and are produced in a profusion of small clusters. The *Yellow Banksian
Rose* has pale yellow, or straw-coloured flowers, in
size rather larger than the white, being perfectly
imbricated, and really gems of beauty, but without
odour; if either this or the white were to be seen
apart from the plant, by the inexperienced, they
would never be taken for a rose, so unlike are they
to any of the tribe. Travellers inform us that these
roses are cultivated in China, under the name of
Wongmoue-heong, where a pink variety has been
seen, for which as yet we have longed in vain, but
it may now be confidently expected from the many

Horticultural expeditions at present engaged in exploring that hitherto sealed country.

~~~~~~~~~~~~~~~~~~~~~~~~~~~~

ROSA MULTIFLORA.

THE MULTIFLORA ROSE

Is a native of Japan, and is consequently more hardy than the preceding family. Its name is as familiar to the ear as that of the rose itself. It was among the first that ever had any celebrity in this vicinity, and I have no doubt of its having been cultivated in this country thirty years ago. In dry soils it is tolerably hardy, and south of this perfectly so. The flowers are produced in such profusion that it has often received the cognomen of *wreath-rose.* The treatment and pruning may be the same as recommended for Rosa Sempervirens. Several varieties have been produced from it, which in some instances rivalled the original. *Alba* is a blush white, in every character similar to the following, except in colour. *Multiflora* is the name of the oldest cultivated sort. The flowers are perfectly double, cupped shape, produced in clusters of a pretty pink colour, about an inch in diameter. When first brought into notice about Philadelphia, it is said that twenty dollars were frequently given for a single plant. Floriculture has now more patronage, and thousands of admirers, so that the grower can afford to put every article at a very low rate; indeed many roses, and even the one in question, can be purchased for as many cents, so that for this trifle every garden in the land may have a rose. *Grevillia,* or Seven Sisters, was at one period greatly esteemed and admired for its variety of character; although its singularity is still the same, yet its former admirers have transferred their encomiums to other more beautiful sorts. It is a fine grower, producing its flowers in large clusters, not two of which are alike; opening of every shade, from pure white to deep purple. Indeed this rose has no compeer; it produces its flowers single, semidouble, and double, and in such variety of shade and colour, that there are rarely two alike. An east or northeast situation suits it best; otherwise the effect of its variety is greatly diminished by the direct rays of the sun. It requires a dry sheltered spot. *Laure Davoust* is the climax of perfection in this family; with all the aid of the imagination its beauty on a well grown plant cannot be pictured. The flowers are of various shades of colour, from white to a lovely deep pink, perfect in form, the clusters are immense, and produced from almost every eye of the strong wood of the preceding year; it is of very strong growth, making shoots of twenty feet in one season, with very luxuriant foliage, and is more hardy than the three former.   For covering outbuildings, verandahs, columns, temples, &c., it has no superior.   *Russelliana*, Scarlet Grevillia, Russell's Cottage Rose, Cottage Rose, and I believe it is sold under some other titles besides, is considerably hybridized, but not so as to lose its character as a pillar rose, of which it is one of the best.   I have pillars of it twenty feet high, forming, during the month of June, a very attractive object, having a profusion of flowers of the richest shades of crimson ; many of them being striped with white.   From the base to the pinnacle it is one mass of glowing beauty. Perfectly hardy in our coldest latitudes, it has large rich green foliage, very distinctly and deeply nerved, the shoots are strong and erect, and will grow freely in any soil or situation.   The old shoots only should be thinned out ; the young wood ought never to be shortened unless locality demands it.   The same style of pruning will apply to all the varieties of the Multiflora.   This operation should be performed early in the spring, before the buds swell, but never when the wood is in a frozen state.   In more southern climates pruning can be done at any period, from December to January ; but in the middle and eastern states it should be undertaken as soon as frost is out of the wood, in February or March, and the plants tied or nailed at once to their respective supports.

~~~~~~~~~~~~~~~~~~~~~~~~~~~~~~

HYBRID CLIMBING ROSES.

UNDER this head I have to place several sorts that have made their appearance, partaking of the habits of other families, but which, notwithstanding, cannot be properly classed with them. It is always a difficult point to decide on the connecting link between the various species and varieties of the rose; they have now become so numerous by hybridization, sports, and other speculative features, that in many instances there is doubt where to place many choice sorts that are almost yearly brought to our notice. I will, however, in no instance, follow the path of others, merely because the track is made, but will, from observation, make all my own assertions, and give my own views, trusting that my readers will make allowances for soil, climate, and a difference of opinion on all subjects.

Garland is a pretty white, producing its flowers in clusters, containing frequently from seventy-five to one hundred, forming a conical corymb of about sixteen inches in diameter, the whole plant appearing in the distance like a pagoda of snow interspersed with foliage of the brightest green; the growth is very rapid, making ten to twelve feet in a season. *Madame d'Arblay*, or Wells' White Climber, has been highly extolled; in growth it is the giant of climbers, for strength and rapidity excelling any that I have seen; the foliage is also very strong, partaking, in that respect, of the Bourbon family. Its flowers are pure white, like the preceding, and produced in very large bunches. It is of a very hardy nature, and will withstand severe cold without being the least affected. For covering arches, arbours, or such erections, it has no equal: there is no doubt of its also being an excellent variety to propagate for stocks whereon to bud or graft the finer sorts of Bengal, Tea, or Bourbon Roses, having no appearance of being liable to sucker from the root.

Ruse Blanche, or Bengalensis Scandens, is apparently a hybrid between some of the Sempervirens and Tea family; its very large flowers, about three and a half inches in diameter, perfectly double, of a waxy blush colour delicately suffused with white, are objects of great attraction, and admired wherever seen; it is moreover a very early rose. Whoever has visited the celebrated

Bartram Garden, near this city, about the end of
May or first of June, must have been struck with
its beauty there, spreading nearly over the whole
side of the dwelling, and covered with thousands
of pendulous blushing beauties. The variety of
names under which it is cultivated (even by indi-
viduals that ought to *see* better) is really amusing.
Rose and White Noisette, Striped Noisette, Indica
Major, Walton Climber, a *new* rose from Natchez,
and some others, of which I have no note. *Ruga*,
or Tea Scented Ayrshire, is evidently a variety
between the Tea Rose and the celebrated Ayrshire
Rose, having the growth and habit of the latter,
with a considerable portion of the delightful fragrance of the former; it is of the most delicate
blush colour, and tolerably double; a profuse
bloomer, and seeds freely. It does well as a pillar
Rose, but has not wood nor foliage sufficient for
covering walls or arbours. *Astrolabe, Elegans,
Hybrida*, and some others of this class are not
worth attention; all these roses bloom only once in
the season, but are of considerable duration, say
six weeks in cool seasons, but if in severe heat,
their time of inflorescence will not exceed one
month. The pruning and training recommended
for Rosa Sempervirens will suit these. They are all
fragrant, and a rosary cannot be complete without
them. To grow them in perfection they require

3

rich ground on a dry bottom; in such a situation, after being well established, they will make shoots twenty feet long in one season.

~~~~~~~~~~~~~~~~~~~~~~~~~~~~

ROSA RUBIFOLIA.

THE PRAIRIE ROSE.

THIS native is destined to convey to every hall, cottage, and wigwam of the Union, the Rose, the acknowledged queen of flowers. Its constitution is such that it will bear without injury the icy breezes of the St. Lawrence, or the melting vapours of the Mississippi. It was in 1837 that we first saw a double variety of this rose, although such has been cultivated in Ohio and Kentucky for many years. The flowers are produced in large clusters of various shades of colour from blush to deep rose, blooming with us from the end of June to the end of July, being a period of the year when there are few others in a flowering state, thereby filling up a space between the first and second blooming of the Noisette, Tea, and Bourbon families. The foliage is rough, large, and generally of a dark green; the wood is strong and flexible, and for rapidity of growth has no equal.

I have no doubt that in good soil it would reach one hundred feet in a very few years. It is admirably adapted for covering rock work, old buildings, or any other object requiring to be hid; it also delights in a procumbent position, and can be used for covering naked spaces of rough ground, or even to make a flowery carpet of every shade of colour. For the following varieties we are indebted to Mr. Samuel Feast, Nurseryman, Baltimore, who raised them from seeds of the native Prairie Rose. There is not a rose fancier but will thank him for opening a field for the hybridizer, in which the rose is to be cultivated to admiration, and blooming six months of the year, throughout every state of the Union. These roses will form parents to be impregnated with the more fragrant blooming sorts, such as Bourbon, Tea, Bengal and Noisette. We may therefore expect from them a progeny perfectly hardy, and blooming at least three or four times during the season. In general, rose-growing is confined to latitudes south of 41°; the Chinese varieties, and their hybrids, that bloom constantly, being too tender to bear winter exposure north of that line. When we can produce perpetual blooming hybrids from this Rosa Rubifolia, they will withstand every variety of climate, and perhaps may some day be seen covering the frozen hut of the Esquimaux. *Baltimore Belle* is a pale blush, fading to nearly white, produces a profusion of very compact and perfectly double flowers in clusters of six to twelve.

Beauty of the Prairies, Queen of the Prairies, or Madam Caradori Allan, or Mr. Feast's No. 1, is certainly the best of the group, having very large rose-coloured flowers three inches in diameter, frequently showing a stripe of white in the centre of each petal. They are produced in clusters, in which they always appear cup-shaped, and stand for several days without being affected by our scorching sun. Its foliage is very large, of a dark green, wood strong and of luxuriant growth; its blooming succeeds to that of the Garden or June Rose, and is the link connecting its congeners with that family. *Pallida,* very pale blush, nearly white, perfectly double; this rose appears to bloom finest when lying on the ground; in such a position it forms a solid mass of flowers and pale green foliage. *Perpetual Michigan,* very double, rosy purple flower, quite flat; this variety is said to bloom in the autumn. I have grown it two years, but it has not shown that tendency with me; but I have no doubt that old well established plants will be found to give freely a secondary bloom. *Superba* appears to be the best of the pale varieties, is of very perfect cup-shape, blooming in fine clusters, and though very similar to *Pallida,* is distinguished from it, by being more perfect, and flowering, I think, a few days in advance of that variety. It makes an elegant pillar rose. The above sorts are so very double, that they seldom produce seed even by artificial aid. The variety called *Elegans*, which is generally grown in Ohio and Kentucky, and in some places called *Chillicothe Multiflora*, has been cultivated here for five years; it is not so double, of a pink colour, seeds more freely, and when hybridized by the Perpetual and Chinese Roses, will give, no doubt, many varieties. I have now a few hundred plants, one and two years old, obtained in that manner, which exhibit in their growth great diversity of character, but have not yet bloomed. They are all very easily propagated by layering in July: give the shoot of the present year's growth a twist, and then bury the twisted part six inches under ground; in November it will be well rooted, and can then be cut off and transplanted in any desired situation; the tasteful husbandman may thus cover every unsightly fence rail.

Having briefly disposed of the tribes of Climbing Roses that bloom only once in the season, a few hints on their general culture will be in place.

They will grow luxuriantly on any aspect or situation, provided they are not entirely shaded by trees over head. The roots of trees and plants gene-

rally are of a growth proportionate to that of their
branches; from this data, and experience proves it,
we find that roses of strong growth make strong
roots, striking deep into the soil, and extending
horizontally in quest of food to a surprising length;
they require a rich soil, which, before planting,
should be well pulverized and freely broken; it
should be of a character inclining more to sand
than clay; if the latter predominate it must be
well incorporated with sand and old manure until
it becomes of a friable nature. With two feet
depth of such a soil, they will grow many years,
and bloom profusely. When any decline is observed, it will indicate that they are in want ·of
nourishment, which can easily be supplied by digging in about their roots three or four inches thick
of manure or rich compost. For such an operation
the month of November to early in spring is the
best period of the year. Wherever their situation
may be, all the pruning they require is merely to
thin out the wood where it is too crowded, and to
keep it within bounds. I have seen fine plants of
many of the roses now described totally ruined for
one year by the free use of the knife.

Where manure cannot be conveniently obtained,
fresh soil from the woods or rich grounds will be of
great service; an occasional watering with soap
suds is also very beneficial to the rose. In city

gardens we have often seen a few inches of very common poor soil thrown over clay, old bricks, lime rubbish, &c., whereon roses were planted, and grew well the first season, but the following they made barely sufficient wood and foliage to keep them green; the result was unsatisfactory, and the fault laid to the rose; whereas the whole fault was in the preparation of the ground. "Any thing that is worth doing at all, is worth doing well," is a maxim always to be kept in mind in all gardening operations.

ROSA RUBIGINOSA.

THE SWEET BRIER.

THE Eglantine has been the theme of poets and lovers for many centuries. It is to be found in some sort growing wild in many parts of both hemispheres. To the flower there is no special beauty attached, being a very simple looking single pink blossom. Although there may be great beauty in simplicity, yet to admirers of the rose, singleness is at once an objection. The odour emitted by the plant after a shower, or when fresh with the dews of evening and morning, is certainly very grateful,

and even delicious.   Wherever there is a hedge to
be planted, it should have a few plants of the sweet
brier interspersed; it bears clipping well, and even
a hedge of itself would prove a garden ornament
rarely equalled, being of a lively green, and its
many associations will make it always pleasing.
To keep it within bounds, it can be freely clipped
or sheared twice a year, and should not be allowed
to get over four feet high.   The plant grows in
many of our woods, and is described by some
American botanists, although others consider it to
be an acclimated foreigner; be that as it may, its
fragrance and qualities are the same, and familiar
to all.   Growers and sellers have taken the advantage either by hybridizing or natural appearance,
and have introduced to our notice *Double Yellow
Sweet Briers, Double White Sweet Briers,
Double Red Sweet Briers, Celestial Sweet
Briers, Double Striped Sweet Briers,* and what
will come next cannot be divined.   Some of these
are certainly well worth attention, and others are
about as much like a raspberry bush as a sweet
brier.   However, the following may be cultivated,
observing that they have none of the climbing
character of the original.   *Celestial,* very pale
blush, approaching to white; flowers small and
double; foliage small, and has a little of the spicy
odour so agreeable in the original.   It appears to

be a hybrid, between the Eglantine and the Scotch
Rose. *Rose Angle* has bright rosy red flowers,
quite double, grows freely; foliage stronger than
the preceding, and equally as fragrant. *Double
Red*, or *Double Scarlet*, has a stiff strong habit,
with very large dark green foliage; flowers of a
dark rosy red colour, quite large and perfectly
double; its habit is quite dwarf and stiff. *Double
White Hip*, or *Sweet Brier;* this is too different
from the original to be classed with it; they are
remotely connected. The growth is very strong;
we have plants seven feet high, making a very
superb pillar; the foliage is large, of a pale silvery
green; the flowers are very perfectly cupped, of a
rose-white colour, pendulous, profuse and graceful.
The Double Yellow Sweet Brier* will be nearly as
difficult to find as the Yellow Moss; all I have seen
with that name are mere interlopers, being the Rosa
Harrisonii, Williams' Yellow Scotch, and some not
even meriting the name of yellow. Strong shoots
of the common sweet brier make very good stocks,
to bud or graft upon, and are extensively used in
England for that purpose.

* The Austrian Brier, or, as it is called, *Single Yellow Sweet
Brier*, is very common in many old gardens. The flowers are
equally as bright as the Harrisonii, with one side of the petals,
in certain stages, inclining to red.

ROSA LUTEA.

THE YELLOW AUSTRIAN ROSE.

BOTANISTS do not appear to agree in considering Rosa Lutea and Rosa Sulphurea as distinct species. But we will proceed regarding them as one. There are hundreds, if not thousands, of varieties of the rose family cultivated; among such a progeny it is rather remarkable that there are so few yellow, and none black; yet there are no two colours more sought for. The *Rosa Sulphurea*, or Double Yellow of Lindley, has never been seen in a single state. It is a very old inhabitant of the gardens of Europe, though comparatively rare here. In Scotland, twenty-five years ago, I saw a plant of it, which was then considered a great curiosity, though it appeared to have been there a quarter of a century; it always showed a profusion of buds, but rarely a well blown flower; it never felt the pruning knife, being left to nature. History first notices it as being cultivated in Turkey. Nothing of its origin is as yet known, though supposition gives it a locality on the fertile soil of the Chinese empire. This rose has produced a great deal of money to the French venders, especially those charlatans who make their market in strange places, where they never intend to appear again under the same name.   This rose has travelled from east to west as the *Double Yellow Provins, Double Yellow Moss,* &c.   The foliage is small, of a pale yellowish-green, the wood rather slender and weak, studded with small thorns; the branches spreading. There is a large plant of it that has been in the garden of the late Henry Pratt, Esq., near this city, for perhaps thirty years, and has never been known to produce a perfect flower.   It is said that the gardens of Florence, Leghorn, and other parts of Tuscany, produce this rose in perfection, which proves that it requires a dry rich soil and an even temperature to bring it to perfection.   The *New Double Yellow, Williams' Double Yellow,* and *New Double Yellow Sweet Brier,* is only a half double rose, of a very pale sulphur colour, about an inch and a half in diameter; a profuse bloomer, and of rather weak growth.   It is said to have been grown from the Yellow Austrian, although I think it is more likely from a Scotch rose impregnated with that variety. It produces seed freely, and its capsule has more of the appearance of the Scotch than the Austrian Rose.

Harrisonii, Hogg's Yellow, Yellow Sweet Brier.—This very beautiful yellow, and in fact the *only yellow* rose of this character that I have

seen worth cultivating, was grown by a Mr. Harrison, near New York, about twenty years ago, and
is evidently a seedling from the Yellow Austrian; its
growth, after being well established, is quite luxuriant, often making shoots six feet long in one
season.   The wood is of a dark reddish brown
colour, with strong straight thorns, the foliage
small, of a dark rich green; the flowers open of a
beautiful globular form, and appear like as many
golden balls; when open they are about two inches
in diameter, and nearly double, blooming very early
in the season, and in great profusion; it seeds rather
sparingly, but will no doubt produce many fine
varieties.   It delights in a good deep loamy soil,
although it may grow in any soil or exposure;
seeds saved from it should be sown and protected
with the greatest care, and at no distant period
we may anticipate, from this very plant, yellow
roses possessing all the requisites of colour and
form that the amateur can desire.   The pruning
must be done very sparingly; if the plant gets
crowded, thin out the branches; the overgrown and
straggling shoots can be shortened to any required
length.

ROSA SPINOSISSIMA.

THE SCOTCH, OR BURNET ROSE.

THIS species of the rose takes its name from its being very thorny. It is in habit very much assimilated to the yellow roses, though of a more spiny or thorny nature. It has been found growing in many of the Alpine districts of Europe, though it is generally known as the Scotch Rose, deriving its name from the fact of the first introduction of it in a double state having been by the Messrs. Browns, nurserymen, of Perth, (Scotland.) As a stimulant to rose growers, I will relate what I have heard from the lips of Mr. Robert Brown, who is now living near this city, and is the very individual who planted the seeds and distributed thousands of this rose through the floricultural world. He says, that "in or about the year 1793 he introduced to his nursery, from a hill in the neighbourhood, seeds saved from this rose, which produced semi-double flowers, and by continuing a selection of seeds, and thus raising new plants every year, they in 1803 had eight good double varieties to dispose of; being white, yellow, shades of blush, red and marbled; from these the stock

4

was increased, and hundreds of varieties obtained which have been diffused over all Europe." Several of them are cultivated in this country. We may safely assert that this patriarch of horticulture was the first to grow roses from seed on a grand scale half a century ago. He still lives in the enjoyment of all his faculties, retaining at his advanced age much of his former originality of mind, and to him I am indebted for the communication of many practical facts, the result of his long and valuable experience. The original varieties of this rose are not esteemed by amateurs in this country. In my fifteen years practice as an American nurseryman I have not sold fifty plants of it; but recent hybrids have given some of them a tendency to bloom three or four times during the season, causing them to be more admired, which will be noticed under the head of *Perpetual Roses.* In pruning, treat it as described for the Yellow Rose.

ROSA CENTIFOLIA.

THE PROVINS, OR CABBAGE ROSE.

This very celebrated and justly popular rose has been an inhabitant of English gardens for nearly three hundred years; its native country is rather obscure, though vague tradition says it comes from the east, a term of great breadth and length; however, Bieberstein asserts having seen it grow on the Caucasus. Some suppose that this is the rose mentioned by Pliny as being a great favourite among the Romans. In this taste the modern world still agree, for it disputes the palm of beauty with its sisters of the present day; although it has been crossed and amalgamated with many others, none of the progeny outvies the parent in size, beauty, perfection, and fragrance. In the humid air of Britain, it blooms, for two months in the summer, around almost every cottage; but with us, two or three weeks in June display every flower, and if the weather is very hot, they flower and fade in a day. I confess that there is great difficulty in deciding on the varieties that do belong to this species, but as we intend to describe only the finest, the specific character will not affect the quality. The *Provins* or *Cabbage* Rose takes its name from a town about twenty leagues from Paris, where it is extensively grown for distilling; *Cabbage*, from the form of the rose, being of a large round cupped form, never expanding flat. Some suppose that its name is *Provence*, from a province in the south of France, of which it is said to be a native; the authority is rather vague, and not adopted by the scientific. The colour is a clear delicate pink, the wood strong, distantly studded with thorns. The *Unique,* or *White Provins,* is a sported branch from the old variety, differing in colour, and also in the shape of the flower, being weaker, having the petals more crumpled, and not so cupped; the colour is pure white, though it is liable to sport, for I have seen it a pretty blush, and in some instances striped and margined. *Belgic,* or *Dutch Provins,* is even larger than the cabbage, being four to five inches in diameter; colour red; buds large and very splendid, and is the most common rose in the country—called the *Cabbage Rose,* from which it differs very materially in the wood not having such strong prickles, though of more free growth; the flower also expands fully, which the cabbage never does. *Duchesne* is a large blush, and a good bloomer, with well formed flowers. *Duchesse d'Orleans* is perhaps a little hybridized, and is a very splendid variety, of a bright rosy pink colour, inclining to blush towards the edge. It is a good grower and free bloomer. *Belle Ruineuse* is a beautiful light blush pink, very double, and finely cupped. *Cricks,* or *Yorkshire Provins,* has very much the appearance of the old Cabbage Provins, though a shade darker, and opens its flowers more freely. *Crested Provins,* frequently, though erro-

neously, called *Crested Moss*, is the very best of
the group; its striking peculiarity consists in the
green silken mossy fringe surrounding the sepals of
the calyx, as it were, half enveloping the bud—a
regular moustache, far more elegant and beautiful
in the estimation of refined taste than any of those
worn by the exquisites of the day. Its bright rosy
pink buds are large, the bloom opening very perfect and pendant. If grown on a standard, about
two to four feet high, the beauty is improved. This
very curious rose is said to be a sport from the
Provins Cabbage, and when fully expanded it
might be taken for a fine variety of such, though
the foliage is stronger, and of a better colour than
the original. *Reine Caroline* may be placed with
the provins, and will vie in beauty with any. It is
desirable from its being about two weeks later than
any of the preceding; the flower is large, colour
deep pink, varying to blush. It grows freely, and
is a great bloomer. *Grand Bercam* is among the
darkest, being a deep rose colour; flowers quite
large, though not so perfect as some others. The
Provins Rose has undergone so much hybridizing
by cultivators, that it has, in many instances, been
eclipsed in colour, growth, and habit, though few
will say that it is excelled in beauty of form. The
striped and hybrid varieties from it will come under
their proper heads, the best of which will be fully

4*

described. They require a free rich loamy soil; close pruning, that is shortening the shoots of the preceding year to three or four eyes, keeps them in the best order; choosing the month of February for the operation.

~~~~~~~~~~~~~~~~~~~~~~~~~~~~

ROSA CENTIFOLIA, *var.* MUSCOSA.

THE MOSS ROSE.*

THIS much admired rose is unquestionably a mere variety of the Provins; although its origin remains in obscurity, it has been repeatedly proven to produce flowers, without any moss, on either buds, leaves, or branches. In 1836 a plant in my nursery had a large shoot on it that sported back to the Provins, and entirely destitute of its mossy coat. I believe that Sir James Smith mentions, in "Rees's Cyclopædia," that in Italy it loses its mossiness almost immediately through the influence of climate. It was first noticed about the years 1720

* In very cold latitudes, where the thermometer falls frequently below zero, all the Moss Roses are better for being protected by dry leaves or a mat, except Luxembourg and the Perpetual White, which, I am informed, stand our most rigorous winters.

to 1724, and is mentioned by Miller in 1727.
There is no rose that has been, and is still so
highly esteemed as the Moss. It is figured and
emblazoned in every quarter of the globe; every
rose that has the word *moss* attached to it increases
in value, and this fact has brought many under this
head having very little of its character; and among
them all it is questionable if there is one so very
beautiful in bud as the common Moss Rose, generally known under the name of *Red Moss,* in con-
tradistinction, I suppose, to white, for it is not red;
it is purely rose-colour, and in bud is truly lovely,
but when full blown it has no peculiar attraction.
Blush Moss is in colour as its name indicates.
The *Crimson, Damask,* or *Tinwell Moss* is, when
opening, a shade deeper in colour than the common
Moss, the foliage larger, wood stronger and more
mossy, and if the old Moss Rose has a competitor,
it is in this. *Angelique Quetier* is a strong growing plant, with rather singular foliage; the flowers
are very double, of a cherry red colour. *Louise
Colet* is quite a new variety, with a double flower,
of a delicate rose colour. *Rouge, Rouge de Luxembourg Ferrugineuse, Vieillard* and *Luxembourg
Moss;* this brilliant Moss is known under all these
names, and like all fine roses, it has many synonymes; the flowers are bright red, imbricated, and
perfectly double; the whole plant is very mossy,

and has a brown appearance; it is a free grower,
and appears to do better in this climate than any
of the others; it seeds profusely without artificial
means. I have several plants from it without any
mossy appearance, and others distinctly mossy.
Malvina is also a free seeder; the flowers are
pink, very compact, but it will never gratify the
nasal organ. *Prolifere,* or *Mottled Moss,* is a
very free bloomer, though the mottled part of its
character is not easily detected. It grows freely,
and forms a fine variety of a deep rose colour.
Oscar Foulard is yet a rare variety, and sells in
Paris at eight francs; it is very pretty, with compact flowers of a rosy violet colour; the plant is
very mossy, and blooms profusely. *Pompon Feu,*
a very expressive name for this bright red miniature rose. It is highly prized by the French, and
is now (1843) the highest prized Moss on their
catalogues. It appears to grow well with us, but
will never be admired at a distance. *Ponctuée*
is only a half double rose, but beautifully spotted
with white, and if impregnated with others, will
make an excellent variety from which to grow
new sorts. *Provins Moss,* or *Unique de Provins,*
is a fac simile of the old Unique, or White Provins
Rose, only mossed; its habit is similar, and equally
robust, with large white flowers, blooming in the
same magnificent clusters; it is yet quite rare, but

with the present facilities of propagating, it cannot long remain so. *Perpetual Red Moss;* this long dreamed of, and wished for rose, has at last made its appearance; the wood appears of a very delicate growth, and quite short; how far it is to meet our expectations, remains yet to be ascertained; the French extol it very highly. My correspondent has sent me a few plants, at a very exorbitant price, one only of which appears to be alive. *Alice Leroi* is another of the very new sorts; in growth it forms a great contrast to the Perpetual, being a very strong and free grower, and appears to suit our climate well; the flowers are large and very double, of a rosy lilac colour, and frequently rose edged with lilac. *Pompon,* or *Moss de Meaux,* is very small, and is the earliest of roses, blooms in clusters, of a delicate pink colour; the plant is very dwarf, and difficult of cultivation, unless in a sandy rich soil, where it grows and holds permanently. *Panachée Pleine,* or *Double White Striped Moss,* has as yet produced flowers of pure white striped with pink, but it may be expected (like many other striped roses) to produce flowers pure white or pink. I have often seen the old White Moss have one half the flower white and the other half pink. *Sablée* is only half double, of a bright rose colour, frequently spotted with red. *Sans Sepales* is flesh coloured, the

edges of the petals pale rose, affording a very distinct variety. The *White Bath*, or *Clifton Moss*,
is a pure white, of rather delicate growth, and
rather deficient in the "mossy coat" so much admired in this tribe. If it had the beauty, while in
bud, of the old moss, it would be an invaluable
acquisition; it is said to have originated from a
sportive branch of the common Moss Rose. In
England, about thirty-five years ago, when it first
"came out," it brought in the guineas at a great
rate. *Laffay's Perpetual White Moss*, or the
Quatre Saisons Mousseuse of the French, is pure
white, and is very pretty when in bud, which it
produces in clusters. The expanded rose has no
attraction, but the profusion amply makes up for
this; if grown in rich free soil it produces flowers
the whole season; in such a soil I have a plant
now (August) entirely covered with bunches of
flowers. On paying a visit to a public sale last
spring I saw it sold under the very enticing name
of "The New White Cluster Moss." Such christ-
enings are an injury to both seller and purchaser.
The Moss Rose in this country is a plant of very
difficult culture if not in a rich sandy soil; but if it
is once fairly established in a rich deep loam, it will
make shoots six feet long; when such can be obtained its permanency is sure. To encourage their
growth, fresh soil, well incorporated with manure,

should be dug in about their roots every winter. The pruning must be done sparingly; if the plants are kept low they never do well, often dying off as soon as they have done blooming. I have lost three or four hundred in a single season by over-doing the operation; but if they are kept in bushes four or five feet above ground they will grow admirably; they also delight in an airy exposed situation. Moss Roses in variety are very scarce, even in Europe; no establishment can supply them in any quantity. The new sorts are all budded on the French Eglantine, and form small trees, that require to be kept free from the suckers which push up from the roots, or the graft would be impoverished and die. Rose trees are quite fashionable, but they must in no case be allowed to put forth any shoots below the bud or head of the plant. Standard or tree roses trained in parasol or umbrella shape make very interesting objects, and the flowers they produce are all fully exposed to the eye, and appear as if almost floating in the air.

ROSA GALLICA.

THE ROSE OF FRANCE.

THIS rose takes its name from its great abundance in hedges and other uncultivated grounds in France. Some writers consider it "evidently the hundred-leaved rose of Pliny," so that it must have been long known in cultivation; and it is rather curious that the French should call it *Rose de Provins*, while the English give it the name of French Rose. It is a very great seed-bearer, and has consequently been much used by florists in crossing with other varieties to produce new sorts; the results have been, hundreds, in many instances, more astonishing for their exalted names than for any other merits; yet there are many of the most perfect character, composed of numerous and regularly formed petals, with colours of almost every imaginable shade. The distinguishing features of this family are strong upright flower-stalks, want of large prickles, rigid leaves, and compact growth. The colours vary from pink to the deepest shades of crimson. Nearly all the striped, mottled, and variegated roses have originated in this group; the recent varieties and improvements of character have gone beyond all calculation, and we may safely arrive at the conclusion that roses of every imaginable colour, except blue and black, will be in cultivation at no distant period; and then it will be nothing remarkable to see white roses edged with crimson, and crimson edged with white; even now I confess that to give even a faint description, is a task of considerable difficulty. It is a vast garland, every link of which shines out in harmonious variety; but from this wreath I will cull only those of merit, and which will be always worthy of culture for some good quality. *Africaine*, or *Belle Africaine*, is one of the very darkest; if seen as soon as open it approaches nearer *black* than any other, but soon fades to dark crimson. The flower is very double and compact. *Aurora* is a bright pink, of the hundred-leaved style, grows and blooms freely. *Amourin* has an agreeable rosy blush colour in its imbricated and perfectly double flower. *Baron de Stael* blooms perfectly, and always gives satisfaction, with its pale cherry coloured flowers, which are large and perfectly formed. *Belle amabile*, dark shaded red, always large and attractive, with bold full petals, and contrasts well with the shaded pink flowers of *Bishop. Champion* is quite new, with very bright red flowers, full and perfect, blooming freely. *Carmin Brilliant* is well and expressively named; it

5

would facilitate the love of flowers to a great degree if their names were always expressive of colour or character; but the title is often all the quality the article can boast of. *Chardon Bleu*, or, in other words, *Blue Thistle;* such a name for a dark slatey shaded crimson rose is preposterous; yet so it is. *Coronation* is very brilliant, nearly approaching scarlet, with bold full petals, a profuse bloomer, and perfectly formed. *Duc de Choiseul* is a very distinct article; flowers freely, double, and well formed, of a pale rose colour, with a deep carmine centre. *Elemensie* is another very distinct variety, with large expanded flowers of a rosy crimson colour, growing and blooming freely. *Eliza* is a large blush, finely cupped, and a late bloomer. *Eliza Leker* is a beautiful pale rose, frequently a little marbled, but so very indistinctly that it must have been fancy in him who described it as such. *Eclat des Roses;* there are several roses cultivated under this loud name ; the one before us is a large bright rose, with bold and perfect petals, and always very double. *Fanny Bias*, or *Fanny Parissot*, is a great favourite, and has few compeers. Every one admires it ; the colour is also scarce in the family, being pale blush shading to bright pink towards the centre ; it is extremely double, and is greatly to be admired for its symmetry ; it is a free bloomer.

Gloire des Jardins is a large bright red, fully imbricated, and always perfectly double. *Hortense Beauharnais,* though described as *Rose vif Ponctuée,* is not worthy of that distinction; these faint spots seen in it after close inspection, are too faint to be deserving of notice. *Hercules,* if it had not another quality but its delicious fragrance, should be in every garden. Its flowers are large, and bright red, expanding freely and fully double. *Isabel* and *Prolifère* are the same; very double pink, in clusters and in great profusion; one mass of pretty pink flowers. *Juliana* is also a pretty perfectly double pinkish red, one of those colours that the eye delights to rest upon. *King of Rome, Ponceau Parfait,* and *Theodore de Crose;* this very fine and perfect rose, like many others of first quality, has a plurality of names, and if it should have as many more they will not darken its bright red colour, nor disarrange its very perfect form. *La Favorite* is a bright cherry red, of good habit. *La Négresse,* not so black as its name implies, only a very superb double crimson, very large, expanded, and fully double. *Madame Cottin,* or *Sophie Cottin,* is a very large bright rose, and a free bloomer. *Mohilida* is a beautiful double pink, with a blush edge, very pretty and profuse. *Matilda* is another very handsome pink, and greatly admired; its closely imbricated petals and profusion are great

attractions.   *Nonpareil* is another imbricated pink,
but several shades darker than the former.   *Narbonne* is quite a new rose, of a beautiful cherry
purple, perfectly imbricated, a profuse bloomer,
and of good habit.   *Ornement de Parade*, an
abundant blooming large pink, of rapid growth
and strong habit.   *Polivetis* is a very bright crimson, of the crown form always admired.   *Philippe
Quatte* is a new pink rose, with very large flowers,
having bold round petals; though not so full as
others, yet it is very desirable in a collection.
Pourpre de Vienne blooms very early, of a distinct
purplish blush colour, with perfectly double cupped
flowers in great profusion.   *Queen of Violets* is
an old rose, but as scarce as if it only had originated last season.   The form is of the most perfectly imbricated character, and the colour of a
violet purple rarely met with.   *Ranunculus* takes
its name from being like that flower; it is a great
and persistent bloomer, of very double form, showing a profusion of mottled rosy purple flowers all
over the plant.   *Royal Bouquet* is of a crown form
admired by all; the colour is a bright soft pink, and
for profusion it is equal to the preceding, and of
the same habits.   *Saint Francois* is a bright rosy
pink of very neat form.   *Susannah* is a clear red,
contrasting beautifully with the former.   *Souvenir
de Navarino* is a delicate expanded pink, finely

double, and a certain bloomer. *Tuscany*, or *Black Tuscany*, is not black, but of a very dark rich crimson; in richness of colour it has very few equals, and to behold it in its beauty it must be seen before the sun affects it. Its deficiency is want of petals, but it forms an excellent parent from which to procure seed; for being profuse in pollen, you can always readily obtain it to impart to other sorts richness of colour.

The varieties of Rosa Gallica are very numerous, and every year adds to the quantity; they all do best grown on their own roots; their growth is such as will require to be kept under with the knife, and they bear pruning much better than the Provins or Moss Rose. The best period for the operation is from November to early in the spring; thin out the wood where it is thick, and cut back the young shoots to three or four eyes of the wood of the preceding year's growth. When the pruning of a plant is finished, there should not be one shoot crossing another, and every shoot or branch should stand free and straight. The plants require manure or rich compost dug in among their roots once a year, unless the ground is of a very rich nature; in that case once in two years will be sufficient. If some of the plants are pruned in November, and others in March, or after the foliage begins to appear, it will make about eight or ten days difference in their time of blooming. This practice is often resorted to in Europe, which greatly retards their bloom in cool or moist climates; but with us the results are not so decisive, yet they are quite perceptible. Many of the sorts sucker freely; in such cases the superfluous ones should be removed in the spring, and planted where wanted, or destroyed.

VARIETIES OF ROSA GALLICA.

STRIPED, SPOTTED, AND MARBLED.

To Rosa Gallica we are indebted for nearly all these curiously spotted, mottled, and striped roses recently brought into cultivation. The very old dwarf *Rosa Mundi* is a pure Gallica, and is frequently confounded with the true York and Lancaster Rose, which is a pure damask, and a strong grower; the former is the type of what we are about to describe, and although many have been imported by us under this class, I must acknowledge that there are few distinct enough with other perfect characters to merit the attention of the rose growing amateur; all parti-colouring in the rose is greatly defaced by exposure to the full rays of the sun in a day of June; it is necessary, therefore, to see them as soon as open, or on a cloudy day, when they are in all their variegated perfection. *André Thouin* is purplish crimson, marbled, spotted with rose. *Arethusa* is bright rose, distinctly spotted with blush. *Berleze*, or *L'Abbé Berleze*, is a very double violet crimson, beautifully, though not very distinctly, mottled with rose. *Bicolor* is nearly scarlet, having a pure white stripe in each petal, and when half open is really very pretty; though not fully double: it bears an abundance of seed, and will produce, no doubt, many fine varieties. *Camaieu* is a pretty rosy lilac, distinctly striped with blush white, perfectly double, always opening well. *Fontenelle* is quite new, and a beautiful bright rose mottled with blush, perfectly double. *Hersilie* is a beautiful pink spotted with white, imbricated, and very double. *La Nationale* is of a bright rosy colour, striped or mottled with purplish crimson, but with a shower of rain and an hour of sun its variegation is lost. *Monime* is another very new sort, with very double bright rose coloured flowers, distinctly mottled with light purple. *Malesherbes*, or *Melsherba*, is more of a Chinese hybrid than a Gallica, and is the more desirable, as its growth is thereby improved; the flowers are very double, rosy purple, spotted with white. *Minos* is a very double bright rose, suffused with numerous small white spots, very distinct and perfectly double. *Prince de Chimay* is of a rosy purple, very double, with large spots of rosy white. *Panachée Pleine*, as its name represents, is fully double, striped rose and white very distinctly, and the full length of the petals; but it is so much like the Panachée Double that the two are not desirable in the same collection. *Dona Sol* is a very new variety, with large, very double red flowers, shaded with crimson, and spotted with rose, of strong growth, and will be very liable to run into one colour in rich heavy soils. *Jeanne Hachette* is another rare novelty in this family; the flowers are almost as large as our old Perpetual Jeanne Hachette, but much darker in colour, being a red suffused with crimson spots. *Oeillet Perfait* has created quite a sensation in England, and is now advertised at the round price of one guinea. It is beautifully striped, like a Bizzare Carnation, with rose, red and white, is of a fine globular form, and considered one of the best of the group. *Pourpre Striée de Blanc* is a light purple, with numerous small stripes of white; flowers fully double. *Renoncule Ponctuée* is very double, beautifully spotted and marbled with rose, crimson, and white; nothing in the division like it. *Tricolor Superba* is a double crimson, with large petals, shaded and marked with rose and white. *Panaché Double, Village Maid,* or *Belle Rubine,*

was the first of the fine double striped roses, and
has been cultivated and sold under these three
names; the flowers are perfectly double, and very
like a fine Bizzare Carnation, having stripes of deep
rose, pink, and white, regularly over the petals, from
the base to the apex.

There have been introduced this season from
France, several other roses of the striped kind, but
they have not bloomed to enable us to give a description of them, and the characters generally
received with them are so extravagant (as well as
the prices) that they require to be seen in bloom
before they are served up to the better taste of our
American rose fanciers.

From the above it will be seen that this class of
roses are rapidly multiplying, and with persever-
ance and attention we may raise as fine kinds in
this country as they do in France; for they appear
to seed in great abundance. The variegated varieties do not make such strong wood, generally speaking, as those of uniform colours, and we find that
in strong and rich soils much of the diversity is
lost; it is therefore advisable to keep them in
moderate soils inclining to a sandy nature, and
their characters will be brightened and rendered
more permanent, refreshing the soil every alternate
year with manure or rich compost. The following
sorts seed freely, and can be impregnated with any

other sort that fancy may dictate, selecting those
that have regularly formed flowers without being
crowded with petals, Andrè Thouin, Arethusa,
Bicolor, Village Maid, and Tricolor Superba.
Seeds from these will produce every imaginable
variety, from blush to crimson.

ROSA ALBA.

WHITE GARDEN ROSE.

THE white rose of the gardens has been cultivated from time immemorial. Although the original single white or blush has seldom been seen in
cultivation, yet the double is very frequent, keeping
ward at the door of the cottage, or towering by the
window casements of our oldest homesteads. It
is often called the white climbing rose. It must
have been introduced by our pilgrim fathers—a fit
emblem of their purity, and smiling memorial of
the land of their nativity. It is rather remarkable
that among the many new varieties of the rose,
there are so few whites; and those I will introduce
under this head, belong perhaps more properly to
the Damask or Gallica species; yet I am convinced
they will be more in their place at the head of this

article than in any other division. *Globe Hip,*
White Globe, or *Boule de Neige* of the French, is
an English rose raised from seeds of the common
white, a very pure white, fully double and of
globular form ; a few years ago it was considered
"not to be surpassed," but that prediction, like
many others, has fallen to the ground, and now
Madam Hardy is triumphant, being larger, fully
as pure, more double, and an abundant bloomer ;
the foliage and wood are also stronger. The French
describe it "grande pleine, blanche, creusée:" or in
other words, large very double pure white, and of
a cup or bowl form. *La Belle Augusta* is a
blush, changing to nearly white, fully double, a
strong grower, and flowers profusely. *Princesse
Clémentine* is quite new, and very pure white,
perfectly double, and has in its composition a portion of the Provins Rose. *Reine des Belges* is a
very pure and perfectly double variety, well deserving its name. There are several other whites
inferior to these, and not worth cultivating when
better can be obtained. In pruning they require to
be treated in the same method as Gallic Roses ; but
budded plants, about two or three feet high, are
great beauties; their beautiful soft white flowers
are brought nearer the eye, contrasting agreeably
on the foliage of the plant; they are all free
growers, and require the knife to keep them thin

and in proper bounds; they may in all other re-
spects be treated as hardy roses.

~~~~~~~~~~~~~~~~~~~~~~~~~~~~~

ROSA DAMASCENA.

DAMASK ROSE, OR ROSE OF DAMASCUS.

THE Damask Rose is frequently confounded with
the Provins and Gallicas, which is not to be wondered at when the mixture of the various species
by impregnation is indiscriminately practised every
year, often producing plants and flowers, about
whose family scarcely two judges could agree; but
I will point out a few that still possess all the
marks and characters of the pure species. They
all have that delicious and agreeable odor so peculiar to the "old fashioned Damask Rose," and also
produce their flowers in clusters; they have a long
succession of bloom, and by extra culture two or
three of them have a tendency to bloom in the fall,
and are called by the French "Rose des Quatre
Saisons." They are all distinguished by long
spreading branches thickly set with prickles; the
foliage is strong, of a pale green, and deeply
nerved. *Belladonna* is a delicate pink and a
profuse bloomer. *Grand Triomphe* is also a light

pink, very double, and crowded with bloom. *Imperial*, a large blush flower, rather loose, but a very distinct sort. *La Folie de Corse*, bright rose, large and perfectly double. *Leda* is perhaps not a true Damask, but a very distinct and pretty variety, with white flowers edged with pink, "blanche bordée de rose." *La Ville de Bruxelles* is very double, of a bright rose colour, with strong foliage. *Mathilde de Mondeville* is one of the sweetest of roses, of a delicate rosy lilac fading to blush, and blooms profusely. *Painted Damask*, in some soils may be such, but in my loamy soil it is always rose coloured, and not so well painted as the old *York and Lancaster*, which is often striped, and frequently one half pink and the other half white, carrying out the tradition, that on the extinction of the feud between the houses of York and Lancaster, this rose sprung up, with the one side pink and the other white. *Monthly Damask* is a bright pink, blooming in clusters and repeatedly during the season if in rich ground, and is a general favourite. *White Monthly Damask* is not such a free bloomer as the former; these bear seed freely, and have been the parents of many of the roses known as Perpetuals. In pruning give them the same treatment as directed for the Provins and Gallica roses.

6

HYBRID CHINESE ROSES.

UNTIL within a few years this division of the
rose was entirely unknown. It has originated from
seeds of the Bengal, Tea, and Bourbon roses, impregnated with pollen from the Provins, Damask,
Centifolia, and other sorts that bloom only once in
the season. The progeny is greatly improved in
growth, foliage, colour, and form of flowers, but
deficient in the ever blooming tendency of one of
the parents; this deficiency is, however, amply
made up by the great beauty of the flower, its
habit and diversity of brilliant colours; they present a combination of the grand and beautiful,
which must be seen to be fully realized; for pillars
and trellising they are not surpassed; the wood of
many of them is very luxuriant, growing six to
ten feet in a season; the foliage, too, is always
agreeable, being generally of a rich glossy green.
Others of them are dwarf and very compact in
their habits; in fact they offer every shade of colour
(none yellow, I believe,) from white to almost
black; every variety of growth from one foot
upward. Some of them seed abundantly, and
there is no end to the variety that may be pro-

duced; the greatest difficulty will be in choosing
the best, and if the French growers would only
extirpate from their seed-beds every plant that did
not produce flowers of perfect distinction and symmetry, our perplexity would be greatly diminished;
but instead of retaining only such, they introduce
to our notice some distinguished title with a rose
not worth a name. The group is also being de-
molished, and ranking under "*Hybride de Bengale,
Hybride de Noisette, Hybride d'Ile de Bourbon,*"
departing from the foundation of all these, which
is *Rosa Indica*, or the *Chinese Rose*. To give a
full description of the sorts ranking in the above
characters would occupy more of these pages than
is allotted for this group, and we will content our-
selves with naming the best. *A Fleurs Blanches,
Blanchefleur,* or *White Climbing Globe Unique,*
pure white, as its name indicates, is a very free
grower, flowers perfectly double and abundant.
Beauty Bouquet, very similar to the former, but
not of such rapid growth; the flower is also more
compact. *Becquet* is a new variety, with bright
rosy-purple flowers, perfectly double, and cup
formed. *Belle Parabère* is one of the most magnificent roses for a pillar, making long flexible
shoots, very luxuriant rich green foliage; the
flowers are very large, finely formed, of a violet
shaded crimson, and fragrant. *Belle Theresa* pro-

duces its rich dark crimson shaded flowers in clusters finely scented. *Bon Ginneure*, very bright red, edged with violet, perfectly imbricated, an early and profuse bloomer, beautiful. *Belle Marie*, superb, large bright pink, very double, cupped, and sweet scented. *Brennus*, or *St. Brennus*, is superb; the flowers are extra large, of a glowing red, perfectly double; it makes fine shoots, and is an excellent pillar plant; it is the celebrated *Queen Victoria Rose* of Charleston, S. C. *Blairii* is a very large blush, with a rose coloured edge; the petals are very stiff and bold; the buds and flowers are both magnificent; it is an English rose, and said to be a seedling from the common Tea Rose. *Catel* is curiously shaded with red, crimson, and purple; it is perfectly double, of dwarf habit, and makes a beautiful bush. *Celicel* is a rosy blush, a very abundant bloomer; the flowers are large and in clusters; it seeds freely, and promises to be one of the best for hybridizing with other sorts. *Chatelaine* and *Lanzezure* appear to be one; shaded lilac, crimson, purple, and often very bright red, varying very much according to soil and situation; the flowers are very double, large, and cupped; a strong grower, and makes a fine pillar rose. *Cesonie* is a large rosy pink, perfectly double, and makes a splendid dwarf rose. *Cerisette* is a very pretty profuse flowering bright red, almost approaching a scarlet; flowers rather small, but very double and profuse. *Coupe d'Hébé,* "Hebe's Cup," is a delicate blush when fully expanded, of perfect form, large, a fine grower and profuse bloomer, with large glossy green foliage, and makes a fine pillar plant. *Coup d'Amour* is very pretty and very perfect, a bright rose colour and a dwarf grower. *Duc de Cases* is a large rosy lilac changing to purple, very double, of a strong habit. *D'Andigne,* whether on its own roots or grafted, is a very distinct and curiously marked variety; the colours are a violet shaded purple, approaching the blue more than any other rose I have seen; the flowers are of the most perfect form, and very double; it forms a handsome plant, either as a dwarf or standard. *Délice de Flandres* is a large delicate pink, very distinct, and perfectly double, of strong habit, and very fragrant. *Egérie* is a brilliant cherry red, perfectly double, of rather slender growth, and very distinct. *Emmeline* is of a delicate flesh colour fading to lilac, and quite double. *Fulgens,* or *Malton,* of the French, is a very bright red, or carmine, almost approaching scarlet; flowers quite double, and cupped; the shoots must not be pruned very close, for in that case it will not show a bloom. *Fabvier,* or *Col. Fabvier,* is a splendid pink changing to red; flowers imbricated, large, and very double; the plant forms a splendid pillar, and is one of the strongest growing hybrids. *Fleurette* is a pretty pale coloured rose, very perfect, but perhaps too small for the general taste of growers. *Gen'l Lamarque,* or *Lamarque of Luxembourg,* is a bronzed mottled crimson of curious shades, a large flower, always very distinct, perfectly double, and a strong grower. *George the Fourth,* or *Rivers' George the Fourth,* is an old but splendid variety, of the richest crimson colour, always perfect and fully double, of cupped form, a free grower in rich soils, and makes a splendid pillar rose. Mr. Rivers, of England, a celebrated rose grower, raised this variety from seed, nearly thirty years ago; according to his own history of the plant, it came up in a bed of seedlings, unexpected, and without any act on his part to produce it. This shows that superior varieties may be grown from seeds saved indiscriminately from choice sorts, without the aid of hybridizing, which I will prove still more clearly. However, through the manual hybridizing process great improvements have been, and are constantly being made. *Georgia* is an old distinct variety, being bright rose, with white edge, large and fine, but rather tender for a northern latitude. *Grillony* is a large and superb rose, of a slaty colour and strong growth. *Hybride Blanche* is a small neat white rose, with a profusion of flowers. *Helvetius* is of

a rosy-violet colour, very large, and double to the
centre. *La Nayade* is a perfectly formed rose,
of a delicate rose colour, and a fine bloomer.
L'Ingénue is a shaded dark crimson, very double,
cupped, fragrant, and is a free grower. *La Tour-
terelle Parni,* or the *Dove Rose,* is of a dark lilac
colour, perfect cupped form, a large and early
flower, grows freely, and makes a fine pillar plant;
we have some of such fifteen feet high. *Louis
Philippe* is a splendid new rose, of a dark rose
colour, perfect form, blooms in great profusion, and
appears to be well adapted for trellis work, or high
columns, and has the fragrance of the Damask
Rose. *Lady Stuart* is a delicate pink, of perfect
globular form, very double, and apparently a free
grower. *Lord Nelson* is quite a new variety, a
strong grower, with flowers of a distinct dark
brown velvety colour, very double, and perfectly
formed. *Manteau,* dark purplish crimson, very
perfect, and frequently striped. *Pallagi, Malton,*
or *Ne Plus Ultra,* is a bright rosy purple, and a
rapid grower. *Petit Pierre* is a large mottled
purplish crimson, perfect in form, a splendid
grower, and in spite of the diminutive attached to
its name producing large flowers. *Princess* produces its flowers in large clusters; they are a rich
pink edged with blush; it is a good grower, but
will not suit pillars. *Prolifère* is very appropri-

ately named, being very prolific indeed, one sheet
of flowers, of a dark rose colour changing to violet,
finely and perfectly formed, and very fragrant.
Stadholder, or *Stadholder Sinensis*, of some, is a
beautiful clear pink, very perfect in its form, and is,
perhaps, more of a *Hybrid Provins* than Chinese;
it makes a beautiful standard or dwarf. *Sandeur
Panaché*, or *King of Hybrids*, is unique in this
class, having all its flowers beautifully and distinctly spotted and striped; they are perfectly
double and finely cupped; the plant makes a good
pillar, but must not have its shoots cut short, or it
will not produce a flower; tie the strong ones the
full length, and cut out the weak or old wood.
Tuscany, or *Tuscany Noisette*, although the latter name would lead us to believe it a Noisette
Rose, is purely a hybrid, blooming only once, producing its rich dark crimson flowers in large clusters. *Triomphe d'Angers* is a very large and
perfectly double shaded purple crimson, an excellent grower and great bloomer. *Vandael* is a rosy
purple changing to violet-crimson, having all these
shades in the same flower, which is large, perfect,
fragrant, and a free grower. *Velours*, or *Violet
Episcopal*, is of a velvety crimson colour fading to
purple, is perfectly formed, a free bloomer, fragrant,
and makes a splendid pillar rose. *Victor Hugo* is
a perfect picture when in bloom, of a cherry red

changing to a rosy-violet colour, handsomely imbricated, fragrant and profuse, a strong grower, with rich green foliage. *Violet de Belgique* is one of those surprisingly large flowers that all like to look upon; its colour is a very dark violet-crimson, although in very warm weather it will open bright red. It will grow to any height, and in one season will make shoots twelve feet long. *Watts' Celestial* is of a delicate rose colour, the petals all curving inwards, forming a regularly cupped flower; it is an old variety that has flourished under several names, viz :—*Watts' Climbing China, Flora Perfecta, Rachel,* and I believe some others. *Wellington* is also an old variety, but retains its fine globular character fo the very last; its rich crimson colour and dwarf habit makes it very desirable.

The above have been selected from the many now cultivated, and we venture again to repeat that there is no plant to excel them for ornamenting lawns, grass plats, fences, arbours, outbuildings, or any other situation. Their diversity of form, habit, and colour, may be exhibited in many ways. Variegated pillars or columns may be formed by planting a pink, a red, and a crimson together, or a white and red; the combinations can be formed to meet the views of any taste. When a strong growth is required the soil should be dug out two

feet deep, and two to three feet in diameter for
each plant, and the space filled up with very rich
earth composed of loam, decayed manure, and
sand, in nearly equal proportions; finish with the
new soil six or eight inches above ground to allow
for settling.   For a variegated pillar choose plants
of the same growth, and plant them in a rectangu-
lar form, allowing the pole or pillar to occupy the
centre.   The first season after planting they should
be watered twice a week in dry weather; if watering cannot be attended to, cover the soil with three
or four inches of manure.   For pillars or trellising,
plants on their own roots are the best.   The pruning of these require to be performed in a very different manner from that usual for the generality of
roses.   Those plants that make very long shoots
should have only about a foot or two of the tops
cut off, the wood of three or four years old thinned
out, and the short shoots or twigs cut in to within
two eyes of the preceding year's growth.   They
require to be tied to a strong post; if permanency
is the object use red cedar or locust for the purpose;
in the country, where wood is plenty, any sapling
can be taken; if three or six inches of the branches
are left on it, the effect will be improved.   Although
rich soil is strongly recommended for these roses,
they will nevertheless do on any soil.   I have seen
them in the very poorest earth make fine bushes

when they can be pruned as common garden roses, only the luxuriant beauty of the foliage, and the large size of the flowers will be lost. It must be admitted that plants, trees, and shrubs, grown and protected by nature, are in their greatest beauty, and bring forth their flowers, fruits, and seeds to perfection; yet while this is conceded, we say that those plants, brought up and nurtured by art, under every exciting cause, to produce the greatest amount of wood, foliage, flowers, and fruits, also require skilful assistance in depriving them of their superabundance, to keep them within bounds, and lead them to the space they are intended to occupy. The period best adapted for pruning is subject to various opinions; but extensive practice and sound judgment give the preference to the months of November and December. Pruning in the spring should be avoided, as the sap is then drawn towards the extremities of the shoots, and when these are shortened the lower buds will be found more dormant, and will require some time to move, whereas by fall pruning the sap in the spring flows instantly to the buds that are left on the plant, which are at once strengthened, and prepared to push out as early as the season will permit. The first season after roses are transplanted they should be watered once or twice a week in dry weather, or should have placed all round the plant, moss or manure, to prevent evaporation, or the sun from parching the earth and drying the young rootlets. It is lamentable to see the destruction of plants the first season, from mere carelessness and want of attention; whereas a few judicious waterings would have prevented the loss.

PLANTING.

WE have advocated November and December as the best period for pruning; these are also the best months for planting all kinds of roses of the hardy sorts that bloom once a year, or what are termed "Hardy Garden Roses," unless the soil be of a wet and retentive nature; in such case the planting should be deferred till spring. The ground must be well prepared by deep digging, and well incorporated with old rotten manure, decayed leaves, or soil brought from the woods. I am aware that some of my southern and western friends will smile at this recommendation; for their soils are from three to twelve feet deep, and will grow roses, without any artificial means, for the next century; but these suggestions are only offered to those who need them. Before the operation is begun the mind should be made up on the proper disposition of the plants: avoid crowding, avoid formality, avoid hurry. Crowding plants together is injurious in every respect; if space is limited choose the fewer sorts, or distribute the inferior sorts to hedge rows or fences, and put only the best that can be had where they are to form a permanent attraction; formality of design attracts attention for a time, but the eye soon wearies of it. The most interesting disposition, and one that will offer the greatest variety, is to plant the whites, blushes, pinks, roses, reds, crimsons, and purples, each into separate clumps, figures, or patches; and to carry out a grand arrangement let each division of the rose have its appropriate locality. This ROSARY can be formed on any piece of ground, from a quarter of an acre to any required extent, either on the lawn or any other spot for the purpose. Let the ground be laid down in grass, or if it is there already so much the better; then cut out on the grass the various figures that may be required, giving every plant from two to four feet of room. With these few hints the reader will see that such an arrangement will form a scene of enchantment that language cannot portray. It is not necessary to remove the old soil; very decayed manure (with an addition of road or river sand to

7

heavy soils) well incorporated with it, twelve to
eighteen inches deep, is all that is required.

GROWING ROSES FROM SEED.

To the amateur this opens a field of very interesting amusement; it gives an object with which
to fill up profitably every leisure moment, in impregnating, saving the seed, sowing and watching
every movement of the plant till it develops its
beauties of inflorescence, which, if it prove of new
character, is an ample compensation for the time
spent upon the process; if not worthy, it is at least
a good stock to be used in budding or grafting
upon, and even then causes no loss.   In the centre
of many roses there is a number of thready fila-
ments surmounted by what botanists term anthers;
these are small oval forms which, when ripe, con-
tain a quantity of pollen or yellow dust, which can
easily be perceived between the finger and the
thumb after giving them a gentle pressure.   This
pollen, though to the naked eye a fine powder, and
light enough to be wafted along by the air, is very
curiously formed, and varies very much in different

plants. Under the microscope each grain of it in
the rose is a membranous round bag, which remains entire, and can be kept dry and perfect for
days and weeks. On its application to the moist
tip of the pistil (which in the rose is a stiff protube-
rance in the very centre of the flower) it bursts
with great force. When flowers are designed to
be operated upon, the one intended to produce the
seed should be deprived of its anthers early in the
morning, which can readily be done with a pair of
fine scissors; then during the day, or within two
days, take a fine camel hair pencil, and obtain,
about noon, the pollen or dust from the plant or
plants with which you intend to make the cross,
and apply this dust to the pistil of the roses from
which you have previously extracted the anthers.
It will require some practice before proficiency can
be attained in the operation, but a little attention
will insure some success. The organs are fit for
the operation when the pistil has a glutinous appearance on its summit, and the pollen is dry and
powdery. The flowers may be one or two days
old; rain is fatal to the operation—dry weather,
therefore, must be chosen. Patience and assiduity
can accomplish wonders in this department of rose
culture; the persevering efforts of the French cultivators have been so very successful within the
last ten years that we do not at all despair of

seeing a yellow Moss, a yellow Provins Rose, or even striped roses, combining every shade from white to black, and there is no reason why there should not be produced a perpetual blooming climbing Moss Rose of any colour at present known in the family of the rose. Ten years ago we had no idea of a Noisette Rose of as fine a yellow as Harrisonii, and as large as Noisette Lamarque; such Chromatella, or the Cloth of Gold, is *said* to be; perhaps ere this work is through the press the plants in my possession will be in bloom, to prove or disprove the assertion.

The seeds will be ripe about the first of November, and can be retained in the capsule or fruit till the time of sowing, taking the precaution to bury them in sand, where they will be safe from the depredations of mice, who are very fond of them. Early in the spring choose a sheltered spot in the garden, free from the shade or drip of trees; enrich and break up the soil very fine, make the surface quite smooth, take the hips from their winter quarters, break up the fruit, and sow the seeds thinly and evenly on the soil; take the back of the spade, or a board, and press the seed level with the ground, then cover them with about one-fourth to one-half of an inch of sand; if sand cannot be obtained take leaf mould, or soil from the woods, finely sifted, for the purpose; in dry weather give occa-

sional waterings.   Many of the seeds will come up
the first year, and the balance will make their appearance in the second; the third year they can be
transplanted to beds or rows to remain till they
bloom, which will generally be the fourth or fifth
year.   It is truly astonishing to see the variety
produced—red and white, rose and pink, may all
be seen springing from seeds of the same plant,
and from single to the most double; none but such
as are of the finest form, very prolific, and possessing a good habit, should be reserved for culture.
Our climate is so favourable to the maturing of
seed that there is no reason why we should not
only equal, but surpass, any European country in
the cultivation of this " Queen of Flowers."

The blooming of seedlings can be readily hast-
ened where time and convenience will admit.   As
soon as the young plants have made three or four
leaves, lift them very carefully from the seed-bed
with a transplanting trowel, and put them in pots
of rich light earth; then place them in the shade
and give a gentle watering and sprinkling over the
leaves for a few weeks, when they may be planted
into the ground to remain.   I have in this way
grown plants eighteen inches high the first season.
They will, by this method, generally bloom the third
year.   The seeds are covered with a thick tough
shell, which, if allowed to get perfectly dry, and

7*

kept in that state for a considerable period, will take two years to germinate, and perhaps not grow at all; regular moisture appears to be indispensable for keeping the shell soft and exciting the embryo plant into growth. The seeds are on this account providentially furnished with a fleshy pericarp (hip) to prevent their becoming too dry for germination, while nearly all other seeds do not germinate well unless dried before sowing.

PROPAGATION OF GARDEN OR JUNE ROSES.

THERE are three modes, within the reach of all, for the propagation of these roses, namely, by layering, budding, and grafting. Layering, wherever it can be accomplished, is preferable, and will produce the most permanent plants. There are two methods of performing the operation; the one we prefer is as follows :—In the month of July, or two first weeks of August, look over the plants required to be propagated, and take any of the young shoots that have made eighteen inches or two feet in length, bend them gently to the ground, and make fast by a peg, stone, or block; they will in a few days take a set in this form; then under the part that has come in contact with the soil make a hole four inches deep, and about the same width; have a portion of prepared sandy rich loam (if your soil is not naturally such) at hand; bend the shoot in the hole, and look for a bud so situated as to come about three inches under the surface; then take a very sharp knife and commence by cutting off all the leaves that will be under ground; introduce the blade just below the bud and cut upwards so as to cut about half-way through, and make a slit about two inches long, thereby forming what gardeners call a "tongue;" this should be done at the side or back part of the shoot, and to prevent the tongue from closing introduce a portion of the soil, or a chip of any hard substance, which will keep it open, then lay it carefully in the space prepared, and fill up with the fresh compost, leaving the top of the shoot in as upright a position as possible; to finish, make it fast to a small rod to prevent the wind from blowing it about. The tongue should not be in the very spot that forms the bow, as thereby the branch would be too much weakened; the lower eye of the upright portion of the shoot is the most successful spot. When the whole is done place the stone or block on the surface, over the layer, which will prevent the sun from drying the earth, and greatly facilitate the growth of the roots. In the month of November the layers that are rooted may be taken off, and either potted as required, or planted out where they are to remain, heading down the shoot to within three or four eyes of the surface. Those that are not rooted will have to remain another year; prune them the same as directed for the parent plant. If the operation by layering is not performed in the summer it can be done in February, March, or April, before the plant has begun to grow, observing the same directions as given above. About Philadelphia we have pots made about four inches wide and deep, with a cut in the side wherein we place the layer, and either plunge the pot entirely under ground, set it on the surface, or elevate it as required; if in the two latter positions we water it freely every evening, and cover it with moss or some other litter, to prevent, as much as possible, the sun from affecting it. We also make boxes for the same purpose wherein to lay shoots from the Standard or Tree Roses.

PROPAGATION BY BUDDING.

BUDDING, within these few years past, has greatly increased in nursery practice, and multi-

plied the plants to a wonderful extent; it is the
favourite mode with the French growers, and on
the stock which they use, plants will grow for half
a century. I have seen them in the neighbourhood
of Paris, like large trees, with stems six inches in
diameter, and heads thirty feet in circumference.
To cultivate them in such perfection they use every
kind of enriching matter, which they freely apply
every year. Almost every rose can be propagated
by budding; indeed, I may say that every variety
can be multiplied in that way, and form handsome
plants, when on strong stocks, in one year. For
some of the kinds it is the only resort, as they are
difficult to manage by either layering or grafting.
Some of the Perpetual Roses raiely form roots
when laid, but bud freely. Budding may be
easily described so as to be understood by the in-
itiated, but as it is to the unpractised hand that we
pretend to give our feeble instructions, we will
endeavour to omit no detail, even at the risk of
being too minute. The operation may be performed with any sharp thin-bladed knife, though
one for the purpose, called a "budding-knife," with
a thin ivory handle, is best for the purpose. It
should be inserted about half an inch above the
bud, and passing about one-third of the way
through the wood of the shoot, come out again
about the same distance below it, the cut being as

clean as possible. The portion of the bark in the
centre of which the bud is situate, is called the
shield, and when removed it contains a portion of
the wood, which is to be carefully removed with
the point of the knife, as shown in figure 1 ; if the
wood is dry and does not separate readily, it is a
sign the bud is too old, and it should be rejected.
When the wood is too old or too young, the shield
may be taken off only about one quarter of the

Fig. 1.   Fig. 2.   Fig. 3.

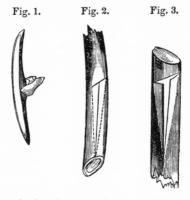

way through the shoot, and inserted into the stock
without removing the portion of the wood it contains ; this method, particularly with very young
shoots, is very successful. If it is necessary to
transport the buds some distance this may be
safely done by cutting a portion of the shoot, and
after stripping off the foliage, wrap it up in damp
moss, a few large leaves, or wet paper, and it may

then be kept for three or four days. In applying the bud to the stock an incision is to be made length-ways through the bark, (but not so as to injure the wood,) about an inch in length, and this is to be diagonally crossed at the top by another incision, as shown in fig. 2. The thin ivory handle, or back of the knife, should then be used to raise the bark, as shown in fig. 3, and the shield inserted within, gently pressing it to the bottom of the perpendicular incision; when it is properly placed, the portion of it above the diagonal cross should be cut off as in fig. 4, and great care should be taken that it is in close contact with the wood of the stock. When this is done bind it up with damp matting, or cotton twist, all except the bud, (see fig. 5,) which must be left free to the air, but protected from the

Fig. 4.   Fig. 5.

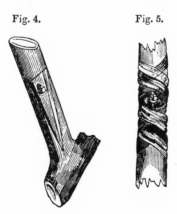

powerful action of either the sun or wet, either of which would defeat the whole operation. In eight or ten days the success of the operation will be known, and in two or three weeks the bandages must be loosened, though not entirely taken away. From the end of July to the middle of September budding may be done, choosing always cloudy weather, or a few days after a heavy rain; but for limited operations any evening may be chosen, always following the indication of the free parting of the wood from the bark, for if the bark does not rise with facility the buds are liable to perish for want of a due supply of nourishment. The buds should always be selected from vigorous young wood that has never flowered. About the end of October the plant should be cut down to within a foot of where the operation has been performed, which will greatly tend to strengthen both the tree and the buds that have taken. In the following spring all the stocks should be deprived of their superfluous wood; observe, however, to leave one bud or eye above the inserted bud, which will greatly assist its growth till it has made a few leaves, and is fit to perform the functions of vegetable life, when the natural shoot must be cut off. As the new plant grows have it carefully supported, for one gust of wind, in a moment of time, will decapitate the most cherished object.

PROPAGATING BY GRAFTING.

THIS method of propagation with the rose is of recent introduction, but is now practised to a great extent by the nurseryman, in the forcing house in January and February, and in the open air in March and April; but in the southern states the out-door work will require to be done in February. The mode now considered as the most eligible is what is termed " whip grafting," without the slit or tongue, generally practised, which weakened the scion of the rose.   The stock which is to be used may be of any thickness under one inch, but the nearer it approaches the size of the shoot that is to be used the better, as it will increase the chance of success.   Cut off the head of the stock at the desired height, enter the knife at a smooth part about three inches from the top, and cut upwards at an acute angle.   Having the scion prepared in lengths of about four inches, take one and slope the bottom of it so as to fit the stock, that the inner rinds of both may exactly correspond, especially on the outer side and bottom; the union is formed first by the rind, or sap, which is directly between the bark

8

and wood, and if they are not placed in contact
failure is certain. Let the graft be carefully held
in its due position, and secure it with cotton twist,
Russia matting, or threads of worsted, whichever
is most convenient; then cover the bandage with
well wrought clay, or grafting wax, which is made
as follows:—Two ounces beeswax, one ounce tal-
low, four ounces common pitch, twelve ounces
Burgundy pitch, all melted together, and used
when warm, with a brush. When the operation is
performed close to the ground, or even under the
surface; after the graft is properly tied draw up
earth all round, leaving one or two buds above;
this method is both convenient, and in many instances preferable, and more to be depended upon.
There are also two other methods of grafting frequently practised, called cleft-grafting, and rind-
grafting, (the former once in high repute,) but the
high winds are very liable to break them off, and
they do not make such a fine finish as the method
above described. The grafts will have taken when
they begin to grow freely; the bandages may then
be unloosed and tied over again, to allow for the
swelling of the wood. Give them a stake for support, tying them thereto to prevent accidents from
the wind. Do not allow any shoots to come up
from the stock. The best kinds of stocks to use

are the Sweet Brier, Dog Rose, Madame d'Arblay,
or Noisette Reuse Blanc. The Boursault Roses
are very frequently worked upon, but they are
short-lived and thin barked. A rose that has a
strong bark is preferable.

ROSES THAT BLOOM THE WHOLE SEASON.

NOISETTE ROSES.

IF in Pliny's time the beauty of the rose was conceded by all, and its praises sung in undying strains by Roman poets, how can we of the nineteenth century, who have seen this gem of nature brought to such perfection, and blooming in endless variety from the dawn of spring to the frosts of winter, sufficiently admire? how can we adequately celebrate its merits? The roses of June, though surprisingly splendid, are past and gone within the space of a month, and even during some of our warmest weather a plant will not be in perfection over one week, unless by extra care and protection. But through the ever fruitful and wonderfully supplying sources of nature, aided by art, we have "roses of all hue" from June to January, equally as rich in colour, and of as pleasing a fragrance as any of those of ancient times. This country has contributed her quota to the grand

Floral Temple, in raising the first plant known under the name which heads this article. The original rose was grown in Charleston, South Carolina, by Mr. Noisette, about the year 1815, and sent by him to his brother, then a nurseryman in Paris. It created a great excitement among the Parisian rose fanciers, and is supposed to have been a production of the common China Rose and White Musk Cluster. Since its introduction thousands have been raised and hybridized from it, till the progeny has become so much amalgamated with the Tea, Bengal, and Bourbon Roses, that the division, I may say, is not to be recognized. We often see a new sort named *Tea*, which, after being fully tested proves to have the habit of a Noisette, of which the leading feature is the clustering of its buds and flowers; it is also either always of a dwarf or a rampant habit. They are generally in this latitude perfectly hardy; all are so in the south, and few or none hardy enough to bear the rigour of our Eastern or Northern States. The profusion and perpetual succession of their flowers produced in immense clusters, frequently from fifty to one hundred in each, makes them superbly ornamental objects, calculated for columns, pillars, fences, or trellis work. Although hardy here, they still are benefited by a light protection of straw, mats, litter, or branches, which should be gradually removed in the spring, after the frost is entirely out of the ground. In the south they require nothing but pruning to keep them within bounds, and if the ground is sandy or poor they must have a regular annual dressing about their roots with very old manure, or some enriching matter. Among the many the following will embrace the best and most distinct. The flowers vary much in size, from one to four inches; I will consider that two inches is the medium size. *Alba* is a pure white, of small size, but blooms most profusely; it never exceeds three feet in height, and makes a beautiful dwarf bush, requiring very little support. *Alzand*, pale pink, very double, with fine large petals, fragrant, and of medium growth. *Aimée Vibert*, or *Nevia*, is a beautiful pure white, perfect in form, a profuse bloomer, but though quite hardy does not grow freely with us; however, when budded on a strong stock it makes a magnificent standard, and blooms with a profusion not surpassed by any; this very exquisite variety was grown from seed of a rose that blooms only once in the season (Sempervirens Pleno) by J. P. Vibert, of Lonjeameaux, near Paris, who has grown many very superb roses from seed. When I visited him, in 1839, whilst discoursing upon roses, he directed my attention with great enthusiasm to this plant, and said, " Celle ci est si belle, que Je lui ai donné le nom de ma fille chérie

—Aimée Vibert." This enthusiasm can be easily understood by those who, like myself, have been so fortunate as to see the two "Aimée Viberts"— the rose and the young girl—both in their full bloom, and both as lovely as their sweet name. In the southern states it grows freely, and is a profuse bloomer during the fall months. *Belle Marseillaise* is a very dark variety, approaching crimson, perfectly double and distinct. *Boulogne* is one of the darkest of the family, approaching a violet colour, though a small flower, yet is very perfect and a profuse bloomer. *Belle D'Esquermes* and *Camellia Rouge* are the same, and is an excellent pillar rose, of a very distinct bright red, fading to a rosy-purple colour; flower above medium size, and though not perfectly double, yet a fine bloomer. *Charles the Tenth* is an old variety, but keeps its distinctive character of colour and fragrance, and is in great demand by the southern rose growers. It does not generally open well with us, but in a warm dry atmosphere, and during our summer months, it shows its large double rosy-purple flowers in great perfection. *Champneyana*, or *Champney's Pink Cluster*, light pink, a rampant grower, profuse bloomer, quite hardy, even in cold latitudes; it is universally cultivated, and well adapted either for pillars or arbours. *Chromatella* has charms of colour, which

to the French and English growers make it very
desirable; plants have not yet bloomed with us,
but will do so in March or April, 1844.   It is described as "grande double jaune, aussi foncé que
notre ancienne rose jaune, couleur unique encore
dans l'espèce," or, in other words, "large double
yellow, of as bright a shade as our old yellow
rose; colour as yet *unique* in the group of Noisettes."   The English advertise it under the name
of "*Cloth of Gold Noisette*, with very large flowers
and fine bold stiff petals, withstanding the effects of
the sun, retaining its colour, a perfect yellow, equal
to the Yellow Harrison Rose."   It is a seedling
from Noisette Lamarque, and very much of the
habit of its parent, with leaves more round, and
growth more robust.   It is very rare, and sells at
twenty-five francs in France.   *Corymbosa* was
flatteringly represented to be a superb snowy
white, of rampant growth, and a profuse bloomer.
I have never seen it deserving such a character,
being a shy bloomer, with twisted sickly looking
foliage.   *Clara Wendel* is another rose having a
yellow shade to its flowers changing to white; it is
of a dwarf habit, though the flowers are of the
largest size, and perfectly double.   It first appeared
under the name of "Thea Clara Wendell."   *Chloris*
has flowers of the medium size, double, of a distinct rosy lilac colour, and is a very fine dwarf

variety.   *Comtesse Orloff* is a bright rosy pink,
and makes a good plant for covering fences, pillars,
&c., being a rapid grower and free bloomer; the
flowers are rather small in proportion to the
growth of the plant.   *Conque de Venus* is now
an old variety, but not often excelled in fragrance
and profusion; the flowers are perfectly double,
creamy white, and with a bright pink centre; they
are produced in large clusters and in great profusion.   *Cora L. Barton* has no compeer, combining size and colour; it is a seedling from Lamarque, grown by me a few years ago; the flowers
are of a clear rosy pink, very large, fragrant, double,
and cup shaped; a profuse bloomer, of strong habit,
and makes a splendid pillar.   *Du Luxembourg* is
not hardy enough for this latitude, but bears full
exposure in the south, where it shows its beautiful
rosy purple flowers in great splendour; it is very
sweet scented, of good growth, a free bloomer, perfectly double, and very distinct.   *Euphrosine;* this
new and very sweet scented rose was first introduced as a "Tea," but after trial proves to be a
Noisette of great excellence, both in its peculiar
rosy buff coloured flowers, which it produces in
extravagant profusion, and in its peculiarly grateful fragrance; the flowers are quite double, above
medium size, and the plant grows freely.   It is yet
very scarce.   *Eugene Pirolle,* or *Admiral de*

Rigny, is a Noisette, of very perfect form; its bright rose coloured flowers are produced in large clusters; it is of a dwarf habit, and makes a fine border variety. *Fellenberg*, as a Noisette, has no equal for brilliancy of colour, during the autumnal months; in the early part of the season, it is of a pale red, but in the fall its colour approaches a scarlet, with large flowers produced in clusters of thirty to fifty. It is perfectly hardy, a great acquisition to this family, and should be in every garden or rosary that has any pretensions to variety; the foliage, when young, has also a peculiar red colour. *Fleur de Jeune Age* is quite a new variety, and has the growth and habit of *Jaune Desprez*, and no doubt is a seedling from that rose; it is of a yellowish-white, with a delicate pink centre, quite fragrant, and has been classed among the "Teas." The Noisette Roses have become so much impregnated with the varieties of Rosa Odorata, that many of the sorts, when they bloom for the first time, are denominated "Thea" roses, but their farther growth and subsequent bloom brings them under the head of Noisettes, from their tendency to produce their flowers in large clusters. *Jaune Desprez, Desprez D'Arcole*, and *French Yellow Noisette*, are the same. It has been cultivated about Philadelphia these ten years past, and is yet a scarce variety. It enjoys a celebrity which few

of its tribe have attained for hardiness, rapidity of
growth, fragrance, and when well established, profusion of flowers, which it produces in large clusters.   The colour is a rosy-buff inclining to orange,
and perfectly double.   It should always be planted
where it will be under the eye, as its colour does
not make it a remarkable object from a distance, a
qualification which Fellenberg possesses in the most
eminent degree.   *Julia*, or *Julia Dante*, is a pretty
pale sweet scented variety, though very like Conque
de Venus; it is yet quite distinct in habit, and the
flowers have a little more of the blush in them.
Julie de Loynes has been, and is still considered,
by some as a Bourbon rose; its foliage does in-
cline a little to that family, but the flowers have all
the character and habit of Noisette, to which I consider it to belong; its colour is a delicate blush
white; flowers above medium size, double and
finely scented; the habit is very strong, (though
not of rapid growth,) giving a profusion of bloom
the whole season.   *Julienne Le Sourd* is a very
profuse bloomer, and if in rich light ground will
produce clusters of fifty to one hundred flowers in
each, of a dark rose colour, and is a beautiful
dwarf object during the months of autumn.   *La
Biche* is still a good rose when first open, of a pale
flesh colour, though almost instantly changing to
pure white, rather large and double, is an excellent

pillar rose, of free growth, and is frequently sold
for Lamarque. *Lactans,* as its name implies, is a
milky white, so pure that I do not remember having seen any rose of so delicate a white; I received
it two years ago as a Tea, but it now ranges with
the Noisettes, and among the dwarf varieties, with
very large and extremely double flowers, which it
produces very freely. *Lamarque;* this is a celebrated variety, now known over the whole country
for its magnificent, large, perfectly double, yellowish-white, pendulous flowers, which it produces in
clusters of three to ten in each. In good dry rich
soils it will grow twenty feet in a season, and in
South Carolina, one of my correspondents informs
me, that their plant, now eight years old, covers a
verandah fifty feet long and twenty feet high, and
is one mass of flowers from May to December.
There is also a plant, in this city, that occupies
twenty feet by eight of a fence that faces north,
where it is influenced by the morning and evening
sun, but the sun, from November to March, never
touches the plant, confirming the opinion that in
winter the sun does more injury to delicate roses
than the cold. This plant does much better on its
own roots than when budded or grafted. The
plant that I imported of it in 1833 is budded on
the French Dog Rose, and makes a very fine
standard, but bears no comparison with the mag-

nificent plants that have been grown from it, although cherished and nurtured in my city garden. *Landreth's Carmine*, or *Carmine Cluster*, is of a very distinct carmine colour, quite double, flowering profusely from July to late in the season; its first buds do not open well, but it is well adapted for a southern climate; it was grown from seed by the Messrs. Landreth nearly twenty years ago. *Le Pactole, Thea Pactole, Thea Chrysanthimeflora,* and *New Yellow Tea;* this distinct variety has only been known a few years, yet it is distinguished by all these names; the flowers are of a pale sulphur yellow, changing to a yellowish-white, as soon as they are exposed to the full rays of the sun; the plant is of a dwarf habit, and will make shoots two feet long, surmounted by twenty to forty flowers; it is no doubt a seedling between the Yellow Tea and Lamarque. *Lee, Monstrosa, Cœlestis, Grandiflora, Triomphe des Noisettes,* and *Carassana;* this plant is shamefully circulated under all these names, and gives additional proof that names are more numerous than varieties; it is a good old rose, of a blush colour, producing its flowers in large thin clusters, and opening very well in warm dry weather, but in moist seasons it does not expand freely, and may be called *hard-headed;* it is a strong grower, and is best appropriated for a fence or arbour. *Lutea,* or

9

Smithii, is a great favourite through the southern states, growing freely, and opening in great perfection, except in time of rain; the colour is of a pale lemon-yellow before the sun destroys it, and is delightfully fragrant, though entirely too tender for the open air in Pennsylvania; it makes a splendid rose for forcing if kept in a high and rather dry atmosphere, but if syringed with water before the flowers are expanded, it glues the petals together, and they perish before opening. When I first introduced this rose I could not supply all the demands for it the first year, at five dollars each plant. *Madam Byrne* and *Cora L. Barton* were produced from the same hip of seed from Lamarque, and are roses very distinct both in habit and colour. *Madam Byrne* is a yellowish-white, with a pink centre, large, and very double; the wood is very slender, but of free growth, and makes a beautiful pillar plant; from the same seed I obtained also a bright scarlet rose, perfectly single, which shows that almost every variety of colour may be produced from the same rose, at the same time, and without artificial impregnation, but by the assistance of art, both character and colour may be greatly improved. *Nankin*, or *Mutabilis*, is of a yellowish-nankin colour in cloudy weather, but when fully expanded, with the sun in full blaze upon the flowers, they are nearly pure white. It is very fragrant, and rather a dwarf grower. *Orloff* is now an old rose, but for growing and producing a profusion of bright rose coloured flowers it has few equals; they are of rather loose form, but very showy at a distance; it is admirable for covering outbuildings or distant fences; it is very distinct from Comtesse Orloff, and more hardy; it will even stand the severity of the eastern states during winter. *Pompone* is also a strong growing sort, with a dense foliage; the flowers are rosy-pink, quite double, and delicately fragrant; it is very well adapted for covering arbours or unsightly fences, being a very strong grower, and clothed with foliage from bottom to top. *Prudence Roeser;* this rose appears to be a complete hybrid, and perhaps more properly belongs to the Bourbon family; the flowers are finely cupped, perfectly double, and of a fine rose colour; it is of a stiff dwarf habit. *Rotanger* is a delicate coloured dwarf variety; its flowers are pale rose, changing to a soft blush, produced in great abundance, and agreeably fragrant. *Similor,* or *Le Similor,* is a very distinct and changeable coloured Noisette; it will at some periods, particularly in cloudy weather, open of the most beautiful bright orange colour, and on other occasions I have seen it a pale blush; at all times perfectly double and fragrant; as yet scarce, it has not been fully proven as to its habit

of growth, but appears to be very similar to Aimée
Vibert, having a foliage partaking of the character
of that of the Tea Rose. *Sir Walter Scott* is
very much like Orloff, with a few more shades of
purple in it, and is more double and fragrant; its
growth is equally as strong, and makes a splendid
pillar rose. *Solfatare* was sent to me, by its
grower, two years ago, as a "superb Yellow Tea
Rose, not equalled," and when it first bloomed it
fully maintained its Tea character, but as soon as I
grew it on its own roots, it directly assumed the
habit of our favourite Lamarque Noisette, with the
young wood inclining more to yellow, and the foliage more pointed; in colour it is a *bright sulphur
yellow;* very large and fully double, with an agreeable fragrance. In France it maintains its character and price, being still (1844) sold at fifteen francs
per plant. When fully established it flowers freely,
and grows rapidly; it is perfectly hardy, and one
of the most splendid of pillar roses; it is equally
well adapted for training against trellises. An
eastern or northern aspect, where it will have a
portion of sun, will suit it best, and fully preserve
its beautiful colour. In addition to this rose holding its character, it appears also to retain, as yet,
its name (Solfatare) unchanged; few choice roses
are so fortunate; I say so fortunate, for it is truly a
disgrace to any vender or amateur to change the

name of any rose knowingly, merely to prevent his brethren in the trade from reaping at once any benefit by procuring the article from its original, source, or to deprive a co-lover and admirer of the rose from possessing the plant immediately, and from enjoying an equal pleasure with his neighbour. American growers are not so directly criminal in this respect, but they are frequently led into error by purchasing from some French importers, who, in many instances, have plants to suit any name or colour. It is surprising that we patiently submit to having the same dose of humbug so frequently administered to us. We are also occasionally caught by our English rose-growers, who in visiting France, pick up the surplus stock of any new and choice rose, take it home, advertise boldly under a new name, and sell it at a golden price. *Superba* is one of our oldest Noisettes, and holds a rank among the first for profusion of bloom, of a pale pink colour, and in splendid clusters from the base to the top of the plant, forming a very excellent pillar variety; it will not exceed seven feet in height with us. *Victorieuse, Pictorium,* or *La Victorieuse,* is perhaps more of a Tea than Noisette, being very like the former, except the clustering of its flowers, which are large pale blush, beautiful and fragrant,—dwarf growing. *Vitellina* is strongly hybridized with the Tea Rose, and

9*

has been no doubt a seedling from Lamarque, to which the flowers bear a strong resemblance in colour and character; although its habit is entirely dwarf it makes a very beautiful plant, when grafted or budded, about two feet high; many of the dwarf growing Noisettes are improved in appearance by this method, especially those that have large pendent flowers; such as standards, are really elegant. The whole beauty of Noisette Roses (which is very great) can only be fully brought out where they are properly cultivated. It cannot be expected that these plants will show their growth and elegant habit, when in flower, if they are merely deposited with their roots under ground, without any system of arrangement or culture. In the first place, the situation must not be subject to inundations of water, neither will they do well on a wet soil; they require what is technically termed a "dry bottom," either naturally so, or artificially made; the soil deep and rich, having a considerable proportion of sand in it, and if not very rich, rendered so by thoroughly rotted manure, or black earth from the woods. Their arrangement can be carried out into many forms, and to any required extent, according to the taste of the cultivator. A very agreeable method is to have them in groups, with the tallest in the centre, trained in a pyramidal or pillar form, and the dwarf sorts forming the base of the pyramid; they may be thus disposed, keeping those of a colour together, or mixing the colours; grouping those of a colour together is the most appropriate method; the eye is then relieved in viewing the groups, by passing from white to crimson, and from crimson to white, whereas if the colours are blended together in each mass, the effect is that of confusion and monotony, without any interest after the first glance. The same system will apply to covering arbours, verandahs, &c. In landscape gardening the rose is indispensable; it can be made to accomplish any purpose in breadth or height, depth or lightness. For detached objects, they are also very appropriate, form most elegant pillars, and if placed on elevated ground, have a very imposing effect. The posts used should be of red cedar, best sapling oak, locust, or yellow pine, and sunk at least three feet into the ground, from four to six inches thick, and from six to twelve feet high; if higher, the heavy winds are very severe upon them. For those that grow only from three to six feet, small rods of any description will be suitable, painting them with a green or stone colour; strong twine, willow, glycine, or lead wire, may be used for tying. In pruning, from the month of November to March, thin out the wood of three or four years old, and shorten all the shoots in proportion to their growth; that is, shoots that have made only a growth of

twelve to twenty inches, can be cut to within three
or four eyes of the preceding year's wood; and
those that have grown from three to ten feet
should be shortened down to two to six feet.   By
this process they will throw out strong blooming
shoots that will flower the whole season.   They
must have every year a good supply of rich compost, or decayed offal of any description, incorporated among the soil in which they are growing;
never plant a rose in the same soil that a rose has
been growing in before; if it is required to be
planted in the same spot, remove the old soil, and
replace it with new, to the depth of one to two
feet.   They delight in a sandy rich loam, on a
gravelly or dry bottom; this is particularly requisite, where the soil is of a stiff clay and subject to
crack during the summer months.   If thus properly
provided for when planted, they will grow in the
greatest perfection and bloom profusely.   It is
necessary to cut off the flowering stems as soon
as they begin to fade, thus preventing their going
to seed except when required, as maturing the seed
impoverishes the plant, and retards the reproduction of a succession of blossoms.   If they are not
wanted to grow to a great extent, cut the shoots
down to within two to four feet of the ground
every season. , The dwarf sorts make very pretty
standard plants when budded, one or two feet

above the ground, on the Dog Rose or French
Eglantine; but the strong growing kinds should
never be budded for standards; they make straggling heads, and never come to such perfection
as when on their own roots.   To grow Noisette
Roses from seed is a very easy process, and its
failure or success can be ascertained in two years,
generally in one.   The best varieties for the purpose are *Lamarque, Camellia Rouge, Cora L.
Barton, Solfatare,* and *Fellenberg;* these planted
together, and assisted by art, will produce many distinct varieties, and will fully repay all the trouble
and patience bestowed upon them.   If it is required
to have them of a darker shade than any of these,
pollen can be applied from any of the dark flowering Bengal or Bourbon Roses.   Of the latter, Gloire
de Rosamond will give great brilliancy of colour,
and is very suitable for the purpose, as it already
partakes of the Noisette habit.   From these suggestions many others may arise to the mind of the
operator, and if acted upon, the results may go
beyond anticipation.

ROSA INDICA ODORATA.

THE TEA SCENTED ROSE.

It is upwards of thirty years since this rose was introduced into Europe from China. At what period it was first brought to this country is to us unknown; but it cannot be less than twenty years since; neither are we aware of any improvement being made upon it with us, or even with the French, who are the leading spirits in every thing connected with the rose. It is a free seed-bearer, and has been the parent of many varieties, many of which excel it in size, but few or none in fragrance. Few growers are very successful in its culture; its growth at times is very luxuriant, and it sometimes makes a shoot three feet long; but such instances rarely occur. The varieties from it, however, are magnificent; many of them, of the most luxuriant character, with flowers of all shades from white to red. The family are nearly all too tender for culture in this latitude without winter protection. To grow them perfectly (and they are well worth extra care) the ground should be prepared expressly for them. They delight in a rich light soil with a dry bottom, and in an elevated position. If the soil is naturally sandy, it will only require to be enriched by manure, or plenty of black decomposed leaves from the woods, in which they will grow in wild luxuriance; but if the soil is heavy and clayey it should be thrown out to the depth of twenty inches; six inches of the bottom should be filled up with rough rubbish, such as stones, brickbats, or branches of trees; over these place sixteen inches of prepared soil, which will allow for settling. Two or three weeks after the bed is prepared the roses may be planted. In the southern states, this operation can be performed in February and March, but with us April and the early part of May is the most proper season. If the bed is made in soil retentive of water it will require to have a drain laid from it to keep the bottom dry, or otherwise it would be providing a basin of water for the plants, which to them would prove a " bed of death" in winter. The only shelter necessary here is a covering of boards, glass, or straw; the latter is a bad protection when exposed to rain and snow, which causes mouldiness about the plants, and even kills them; where glass is not accessible all that is required is a temporary and movable frame or covering of boards, which must be removed as soon as spring appears. Treated thus they will not receive any material injury in this vicinity from our severest winters; but to the

eastward, when there is no green-house, they require to be kept in good substantial close frames;
this can readily be accomplished by lifting them
from the various parts of the garden and planting
them very compactly together in the frame provided for them about the middle of October; if the
plants are taller than the frame will admit of, lay
them in an inclining position, what the gardeners
call "by the heels;" they will require no water till
spring. About the first week, or towards the
middle of April, they must be taken out, in a
cloudy day, pruned of all decayed or superfluous
wood, and carefully planted into the place prepared
for them. By adopting this method, which I have
often practised, every lover of this celebrated rose
in the eastern states can enjoy them in the greatest
luxuriance from June to October. A substantial
movable frame, seven feet wide and twelve feet
long, which may be made of two inch rough plank,
one foot high in front and two and a half feet high
on the back, covered with three sash, can be completed for the small cost of thirteen to sixteen
dollars, and will afford ample protection for two
hundred plants, which will embrace all the choicest
Tea and Bengal Roses, and afford a floral gratifica-
tion in roses worth three times the amount. Such
a frame can be placed in a sheltered situation, and
also used for propagating, from cuttings, all the

varieties of the monthly roses in June, July, and August, without bottom heat. However, where there are only a few scattered plants, they will do very well covered with branches of cedar, a box, or barrel, perforated in several places, to allow the moisture to evaporate. In mild latitudes every flower garden should have a full and perfect collection of this lovely tribe. If my words could paint its beauties, or give any idea of its fragrance, I would not plead for it in vain. But one fault they have, and that is, too much similarity among the generality of them; although a difference can be discerned in all, yet I confess it requires, in many instances, a very discriminating eye to detect it. But the following will be found distinct in colour and character, and worthy of any culture requisite to bring them to perfection. *Antherose,* or *Anteros,* is very double, cup-shaped, of a pale pinkish-white shading to yellow in the centre, grows very strong, and blooms well in pot culture. *Archiduchesse Theresa Isabel,* or *Isabel,* a very distinct dwarf growing white, requiring the shoots to be well thinned out in order to make it grow strong for flowering; the flowers are double and very pure; it might be dispensed with. *Arkinto,* a distinct old variety, of a flesh colour, very double, cup form, grows and flowers freely; the bottom of the petals is yellow. *Barbot* is a new and very

10

strong growing rose, quite large, of a creamy-blush colour, and frequently deep pink, though the French describe it as "a yellow edged with rose;" it is highly fragrant, and an indispensable variety. *Belle Marguerite;* the distinctive character of this rose is easily perceived at a considerable distance, its strong upright habit producing its flowers on short stiff footstalks; the colour from a pale rosy-lilac to a dark crimson, perfectly double; when well grown, a great bloomer and tolerably hardy. *Bon Silène*, or *Silène*, is a very variable rose, with extremely large petals; though not so double as some, yet it amply compensates for this deficiency in the size of the flowers, which are of a bright rose, changing to cherry red, with an agreeable fragrance.   *Bougère* has a great many admirers; the flowers are extremely large, fully double, of a rosy-lilac colour, always cup-shaped, and even fading away in that form; the buds are very large before they expand; it is one of the strongest growers, and bears our winters with very slight protection.   *Boutrand* is a noble rose, of a bright pink colour, perfectly formed, and a free grower. *Caroline* is a beautiful rose, of a bright rosy-pink colour, with finely formed flowers, always blooming perfect, and in great profusion, even five or six in a cluster; it is one of the hardiest, and not excelled by any of the family, having every quality of a first rate rose. *Clara Sylvain* is a large and perfectly formed pure white rose, a strong grower and an abundant' bloomer; one of the best of the whites, giving entire satisfaction wherever grown. *Claudia* is a beautiful creamy-blush, perfect in every character, but a very scarce variety. *Comte de Paris* is greatly esteemed in France, and has maintained its price there for several years; it is yet very scarce in this country. There are at least (that we have seen) four distinct roses cultivated and sold for the veritable "Comte." When once under the eye it cannot be mistaken; the plant is of a very strong habit, with large shining foliage, and the spines or thorns distantly set on the wood, but very strong; the flowers generally perfectly double, are of a pale rose colour, the bottom of the petals inclining to yellow; the buds are quite large, rather pointed, and like Caroline, always expanding freely in airy situations. *Devoniensis* is another new rose; though at first represented as being a fine sulphur yellow, and figured as such, it proves to be a creamy-white, but when just open, in cloudy weather, is of a canary colour; when well cultivated it produces flowers of immense size, and in clusters; it grows freely, with dark green foliage, possesses a delightful fragrance far surpassing the ancient Tea Rose, and is a very valuable variety for either pot or garden culture. It is supposed to be an English variety, but is now sold cheaper in America than in either France or England. *Duc d'Orléans* at first sight, much resembles Belle Marguerite, though it is rather brighter in colour, and the growth not so strong. *Duchesse de Mecklenbourg* is a perfectly formed double variety, of a creamy-yellow before it is deprived of its hue by the sun, whose brilliant rays rob nearly all roses of this shade of colour. *Elisa Sauvage* is another of that description of colour; though very different in growth, which is not so strong, yet the flowers are very large, and make a splendid appearance when forced. *Etienie,* white, with a delicate rose centre, very large flowers, and perfectly double, growing and blooming freely. *Flavescens,* or *Yellow Tea,* pale straw colour, extremely large bold petals; it is very splendid when half expanded, but when full blown is loose and not fully double; it bears an abundance of seed, but we have never produced a good rose from it. This plant was introduced into England from China, by Mr. Parks, about the year 1824. In fresh sandy rich loamy soil it grows very strong, and flowers profusely, but does not thrive in heavy soils. My late partner, Mr. Hibbert, introduced this rose and the *White China* into this country in 1828, and the first plants that were sold of them was in 1830; they are now found in thousands over every part of the United States. *Flon* is of a fleshy buff colour, a large double flower, much resembling Luxembourg, though not so strong a grower; it is delightfully fragrant, growing freely in rich light soil. *Gigantesque,* for size of flower, deserves its name; but deficiency in form detracts from that merit, yet its pale fleshy coloured flowers are very showy. *Goubault* is a large rosy blush inclining to yellow in the centre; very double, distinct and fragrant; it grows freely, and will occasionally produce seed, from which fine varieties will no doubt be obtained. *Hamon* is a delightful rose, with large flowers changing from blush to deep rose colour, a profuse bloomer, and appears to succeed best when budded upon a stronger growing variety. *Hardy,* or *Gloire de Hardy,* is a pretty variety, with pale pink flowers quite double, though not so large as the generality of Tea Roses. *Hyménée* is a profuse blooming creamy white, perfectly double, growing freely in any situation, and quite hardy in this vicinity. *Hippolyte* is another of the same character, but has more of the yellow in it, and more fragrant. *Jaune Panaché* and *Aurora* are the same rose; of a delicate straw colour changing to blush, quite double, and delicately scented; the plant is of a spreading habit. *Joséphine Malton* is a new and elegant rose, of first rate character; the flowers are large, retaining

10*

a cup shape to the last, of a creamy white colour;
the plant is strong growing, and apparently very
hardy. *Julie Mansais* is another new variety,
and though generally approaching a pure white,
we have seen it quite yellow during cloudy
weather in September and October; the flower
perfectly double, retaining its cup shape till faded.
La Sylphide; this new rose possesses every requisite for admiration; it grows very luxuriantly; the
flowers are very large, of a rosy buff turning to a
creamy-white colour, produced in great profusion,
and in either bud or bloom is always admired;
does extremely well for pot culture, and is quite
hardy for the garden. *Lilicina* is an old variety,
but continues very distinct from any others; the
flowers are perfectly formed, of a lilac colour, and
though under the medium size, make up for the
deficiency by their profusion. *Lyonnais,* very
large pale pink, often a fine blush, quite double,
blooms freely, a strong grower, and is a very desirable variety. *Madam Desprez* is frequently
seen in very great perfection; in that state it is a
fac simile of a Double White Camellia, with the
most agreeable fragrance. It is rather delicate on
its own roots, but when budded grows well; in the
south it is greatly admired. An amateur a few
years ago presented me with a plant of this rose
as something he had grown from seed, *very mag-*

nificent, and under a new name; I parted with two or three plants before the error was detected. *Madam Galet* approaches Elisa Sauvage in colour, but the growth is much stronger; it is consequently more hardy, and will grow in a more northern latitude.   *Mansais* is very distinct from Julie Mansais in both habit and colour; the flower is quite large, of a buff colour, with a pink centre, perfèctly double; the buds are very pointed, the wood strong and of a spreading habit, very hardy. *Melville* requires only to be seen once to be recognized ever afterwards; the plant will make shoots three or four feet long, crowned with very large dark blush flowers perfectly double; the foliage is strong, dark green, and deeply serrated; it is quite hardy, and very desirable.   *Mirabile* is another of the newest sorts; of a sulphury-yellow fading to rosy-blush, quite double, blooming and growing freely.   *Moiré* is a distinct globular variety, beautifully shaded with rose and blush, very perfect, but apparently a weak grower.   *Niphetos* is a white, remarkable for its large taper formed flower bud, and till it is fully open is very splendid; but like the Yellow Tea, when fully expanded, it is not at all attractive; the wood is strong, and no doubt it is a hardy variety.   *Odorata,* or *Common Tea Rose;* few or none of the family possess the peculiar fragrance of this delightful rose; its large rosy blush flower buds will ever be admired; when full blown it is not so attractive as others, but will always be desirable for its agreeable odour, though perhaps one of the most difficult of the family to grow well. A liberal portion of leaf mould and sand appears to suit it. *Odoratissima* is an old sort; its name would seem to indicate that it has more odour than the former, but such is not the case; its quality consists in growing and flowering freely, of a creamy blush colour, and in being equally as hardy as the common daily rose. *Pauline Plantier;* this is among the many that have light flowers, nearly white shading to yellow, a character becoming too prevalent in the family, and growers should be cautious in putting forth so many of those whose colours are "so much alike," though they may differ to a nice eye in a leaf, a shoot, or an imaginary shade. *Prince d'Esterhazy* is a beautiful blush variety, similar to Lyonnais, except being a few shades darker; it retains its globular form till nearly faded—grows freely. *Princesse Hélène Modeste* and *Princesse Hélène Luxembourg* are nearly alike, though the latter has a little more of the yellowish colour than the former; they are different in growth, and both are fine fully double roses. *Princesse Marie,* when well grown, will be admired by all; its large deep rose coloured waxy flowers, from four to five inches in diameter, of perfect cup form, which they retain till entirely faded, are not excelled by any of the family; it is of a strong upright habit, and nearly as hardy as the common China rose. *Rêve du Bonheur*, or *The Happy Dream*, is a very distinct sort; the buds, before they open, have the petals edged with bright red; before expansion it appears striped, and when expanded is a creamy-blush; though not perfectly double it is yet very desirable for its distinctive character, and being in bloom before any other of the group. *Reine Victoria* approaches Melville; though not of so bright a colour it is fully as strong in habit, but the foliage not so deeply serrated. *Safrano,* when the bud opens in the morning, is a fine saffron or dark orange colour, and is beautiful; in the forenoon it is blush, and in the afternoon a very poor white not worth notice, and unless you see it pass through these changes you could scarcely believe it to be the same rose. *Soliman* is a large rosy buff, with perfectly double flowers, which, in the cool days of autumn, are often bright rose; it grows freely, and is rather hardy. *Strombio* cannot be too well known; though an old variety, it holds its place, with its large pendulous rose-white flowers, perfectly formed, of a cup shape, and in profusion; it is also a luxuriant grower, and withstands our winters without protection. *Taglioni* is a large rose, of a fine white inclining to pink towards the centre; a hardy strong variety. *Theobaldine;* this new variety approaches the Noisettes in manner of flowering, though not in growth; the flowers are large, of a deep rose pink colour, very fragrant and perfectly formed; the foliage is of a pale yellowish-green; it is yet so scarce we cannot say what its character in regard to growth and hardiness may be. *Thebe,* with every character of a Bengal rose, has the odour of the Tea very strong, and is put in this tribe on that account only; it is of a bright rosy-red colour, of rather dwarf habit, flowers profusely, and quite double. *Thémistocle* is a double white, of perfect form, with the centre of the flower inclining to blush. *Triomphe du Luxembourg;* perhaps there is not a rose mentioned in this little volume that has been so universally distributed over the floral world in the space of eight or nine years, as this celebrated variety; the flowers are often six inches in diameter, of a peculiar rosy-buff colour, and may be frequently seen of a yellowish-white or deep rose, according to season and situation; its growth is remarkably strong, in some soils producing shoots five feet long in one season, flowering freely and perfectly, and is possessed of considerable fragrance. *Victoria Modeste,* in southern latitudes, is very splendid, blooming perfectly the whole season, which it does not do here, except in the months of July or August; the flowers are of a fine blush colour, very large and cup formed; the growth of the strongest habit, and the shoots thickly studded with thorns. *William Wallace* is of a pale blush colour, an extra large flower, perfectly double, blooms and grows freely.

There could be many others named, but their descriptions would merely be a repetition of those given; there are others that pass under very exalted names, though roses of very inferior character. A choice bright red or crimson Tea Rose is still a desideratum; there are several that approach that colour, but are not up to the standard of a connoisseur. From the cultivation of the many beautiful sorts here described we may hope to see ere long, this long expected treasure spring forth to delight our eyes. *Bon Silene* seeds freely, and if impregnated carefully with Bengal *Roi des Cramoisis*, a very fragrant rose, the results would, no doubt, give bright coloured and highly scented roses. The most successful grower of roses from seeds has been Mr. Hardy, of the Luxembourg Gardens in Paris, who annually raises thousands by that process; and there is not a year passes that he does not send forth some article worthy of the name of the grower. The Tea Rose is well adapted for forcing, either in the hot-house or hot-beds prepared for them; they require a temperature of from

60° to 70°, and will flower in six weeks from the time they have been subjected to the forcing process; the atmosphere must be kept moist by syringing ; a good criterion to know the humidity of the air they are in, is by observing the dew upon the plants in the morning; if they are lightly covered with it, showing the pearly drops from the tip of the foliage, it is a good sign ; but if this is not seen every morning, the atmosphere is too dry, and the plants must be freely syringed and kept well watered. Budded plants force finer than those on their own roots; this can be done with great facility on any of the Boursault or other strong growing varieties. In July or August layer the young wood of these plants, (the Boursault,) and insert the bud at once about a foot from the ground ; these layers will be well rooted in October, when they can be lifted, potted, and put into a shady place in any frame or out-house till required for forcing. Mildew frequently attacks them when in artificial heat ; a few applications of sulphur water will keep it down ; but if the airing has been properly attended to, and the water judiciously given, that disease will not appear.   Grafted plants stand out all winter perfectly well with us, if the top is pruned in November and covered with oiled paper, oil-cloth, matting, or any similar substitute, which we remove in March, and frequently find the plants in as good order as they were when tied up.   We take this precaution also with many of the Noisette and Bengal varieties; this is so easily practised that it should not be omitted where there is the least danger.

ROSA INDICA.

THE BENGAL CHINESE, OR DAILY ROSE.

THIS and Rosa Semperflorens, although considered distinct species, have been so completely intermixed and amalgamated, that it is now impossible to define the difference between them.   They have been, since their introduction fifty years ago, universally cultivated, and are admired by all.   Not only the cottager and the great, but the poor inmate of the most cheerless abode, and the lonely widow whose domains extend not beyond the length and breadth of her window-sill—all call in this favourite, to adorn the humble porch, to decorate the fanciful parterre, to throw a gleam of light in the desolate attic, and to speak of flowers that never fade. They are of a very hardy nature, and will endure almost every vicissitude of treatment, but cannot

11

very well bear the winter in the open air without
protection, north of Philadelphia. They will, however, do well to the east by covering their roots, five
or six inches thick, with dry leaves, and two feet
all round; distribute some earth over the leaves to
prevent them being blown about by the wind.
Give them rich sandy loamy soil of considerable
depth; plant in an airy situation, and never near a
tree, or any other bush, which exhausts the soil
and deteriorates the colour of the flower. The
best season for pruning is as early in the spring as
their buds show a disposition to swell; in doing so
cut out all the dead wood, shorten any of the young
shoots that are irregular; the old stinted wood
should be cut as near to the ground as possible;
that the bush may stand free and regularly, thin
all over; dig in among their roots every season a
good supply of rich compost or old manure, and
stir and hoe them frequently during the summer.
The remarks we have made upon the culture of
the Tea Rose will not be misapplied if practised on
the Bengal, though these last are invariably more
hardy. There are about one hundred varieties of
them cultivated, but one half of that number will
give every variety and character, compared with
which most of the others will be found worth
neither name nor culture. *Aglae Loth,* shaded
rose fading to dark red, very double, and perfect

form. *Animated,* is a bright pink, very beautiful when in bud; it is a little fragrant, and of strong growth. *Archduke Charles,* is a noble variety, opening a bright rose colour and changing to crimson; the points of the petals are frequently tipped with bright red. *Arsenie,* or *Arsione,* is of a delicate rose colour, very perfect in form, grows and blooms freely, quite distinct. *Assuerus,* is a new rose, deficient in petal and form, but very brilliant in colour. *Beau Carmin,* is of the Sanguinea habit, a very distinct variety, with dark crimson-purple shaded flowers, quite double, and cup formed, is a free grower, and continually in bloom. *Belle de Monza,* though one of the oldest varieties, holds its distinctive character in producing a profusion of flowers, when first open, of a rosy colour changing gradually to very dark crimson, perfectly double; the plant is a strong grower, and very hardy. *Belle de Florence* is a pale carmine variety with very perfect flowers under medium size, a profuse bloomer. *Belle Isidore* grows rampantly, even stronger than the common China, from which its flowers differ, being more double, and changing from pink to crimson. *Belle Clarissima* has much of the character of Belle de Florence, though darker in colour, and if any thing more perfect. *Bisson a' Odeur d'Anisette,* is a delicate rosy pink, of upright growth, producing its flowers in loose clusters; they are perfectly double, and have a peculiar odour. *Boisnard*, is quite a new variety, of a pale sulphur colour changing to nearly white, and appears to have all the characters of a Tea Rose except fragrance. *Buret*, came out at first as a fine crimson Tea Rose, but when cultivated was found to be an indifferent Bengal; its only redeeming quality being a little fragrant. *Caméleon*, is another of the changeable sorts, opening a fine rose colour, and then gradually changing to crimson; is perfectly double, and a strong grower. *Carmin D'Yebles*, is very appropriately named, being of a bright carmine colour, very perfect, growing and blooming freely; *said to be* "striped with white;" many crimson roses have stripes of white, which in general, is more a fault than a beauty. *Cels*, or *Multiflora Cels*, ranks among the best of the blush roses; indeed, for profusion of bloom it has not a rival; every flower perfect, fully double, and cup shaped, growing freely in almost any soil or situation, and is an excellent variety to force into early bloom. *Comble de Gloire* is a very rich crimson, large and fully double; a free grower and bloomer, possessing considerable fragrance; is one of the best of the high coloured roses; it is yet quite scarce. *Cramoisi Supérieur*, or *Bengal Agrippina*, is universally admired for its brilliant crimson cup formed flowers, perfectly double; it is a strong grower, and should be in every collection. *Don Carlos*, may be mentioned for being represented as a striped variety; it closely resembles the common Sanguinea, though not so bright, and has about as many stripes as Sanguinea. *Duchess of Kent*, is a neat pale pink rose, of a dwarf habit, and rather small sized flower. *Etna*, of Luxembourg and *L'Etna* are the same, and like Belle Isidore has that changeable colour from rose to crimson; the petals are often tipped with scarlet, making it very attractive. *Fabvier*, and *Noisette Agrippina*, are the same, and admired for brilliancy of colour (being near a scarlet) and its seeding qualities. *Gigantea* is an old strong growing sort, producing very large and fully double flowers, blooming perfectly, and quite hardy. *Gros Charles* is a magnificent variety, with large perfectly imbricated flowers of a shaded rose colour; the plant also grows free and strong. *Hibbertia* is an American of fourteen years standing, and is one of the prettiest pink fully double roses we have; though of weak growth it produces large flowers with considerable fragrance. *Indica* is the common variety, and generally known as the *Daily Rose*, from its frequency in blooming, and not from its blooming every day, as some suppose; it is the type of the family. When we say large, we mean larger than this rose (Daily), and when small, we

11*

mean smaller than this; the flower is of a dark
blush or rose colour, and about three inches in
diameter; it grows very strong, frequently making
shoots five feet long in one season in rich sandy
soil; it is one of the best for forcing, and thousands
of it are sold in the Philadelphia market at from
six to one hundred cents per plant. Plants two
feet high are grown from small cuttings forced, and
sold within twelve months. Such has been the
rapidity of rose culture about this city, that fifteen
years ago there were not one thousand rose plants
in its vicinity, and now there are, at the lowest calculation, thirty-five to forty thousand disposed of
in the course of a single year. *Indica Alba* is the
very popular *White Daily Rose* first imported to
this country in 1828, and now spread through every
town, village, and garden of the Union. It is very
much like the old White Tea Rose, though the
petals are not so thick and waxy as that variety;
the plant grows more freely and blooms more profusely; it is also well adapted for early forcing.
Icterose is a new creamy-white with yellow centre;
a very double variety, blooming and growing freely,
and has much the appearance of being a variety of
the Tea, though it has not much of its fragrance.
*Jacksonia,** is another American, grown from

* In compliment to President Jackson.

the same seed with Hibbertia, and is a first rate
variety, producing a profusion of bright red flowers
perfectly double; the wood is strong and very full
of spines; it is also known, under the name of
Hundred Leaved Daily. *La Cœmens* is a beautiful rose, the flower being of the form of a White
Camellia, but of a rosy-crimson colour; it is very
perfect, and greatly admired. *Louis Philippe* has
not an equal for growth, in good soils frequently
making a shoot six feet long in one season; the
flowers are large, perfectly double, of a globular
form; the circumference of the bloom is of a dark
crimson colour, the centre a pale blush, making it
altogether perfectly distinct from any other rose in
cultivation; it will give entire satisfaction. We
have seen it passing under the new name of *King
of France*. *Madam Hersent*, or *Augustine Hersent*, is a fine bright rose coloured variety, very
large, and though not very perfect in form, makes
an excellent display; is of good growth, and tolerably hardy. *Marjolin*, ranks among the finest
dark crimson roses; it produces its flowers in great
abundance; they are large, globular, and perfectly
formed, quite hardy, growing luxuriantly. *Meillez*,
or *Thea a Fleurs Jaune*, has been cultivated here
many years, and though numbers have originated
since, yet none has its character for great profusion
of bloom, luxuriance of growth, and hardiness;

the flowers are pure white, and produced in clusters. *Miss Sergeant* is a bright pink rose, of fine
habit, profuse flowering, strong growth, and perfectly hardy; it was grown from seed by Mr.
Mackenzie, of this city. *Mrs. Bosanquet* is one
of the very best of the pale roses; the flowers are
perfectly double, of cup form; colour waxy blush;
the growth is strong, nearly approaching the Bourbon roses, to which it is related, and it may frequently be taken for the *Queen of the Bourbons.*
Prince Charles is a fine new light crimson variety,
very perfect in form, and, as well as many others of
similar good qualities, is an offspring of the Luxembourg gardens. *Prince Eugène,* is a very rich
crimson rose, being in colour between Cramoisie
Superieure, and Roi des Cramoisies; perfectly
double and hardy. *Reine de Lombardie,* is the
queen of the bright rosy-red varieties; it is of the
most globular form, which it retains to its last hour.
The flowers are perfectly double, and produced
in profusion; the plant grows rapidly, and is quite
hardy. There is not a rose of the colour better
adapted for forcing or growing in pots, for the
parlour or green-house. *Roi des Cramoisis* was
brought by me, in 1839, from Paris, where I saw
the original plant, around which there was a regularly trodden path made by its admirers, of which
I was one, never before having seen a dark rich

crimson rose with so much odour; the flowers too were large, fully double, and cup formed; the plant three or four feet high, and fully loaded with its gorgeous flowers. It has since appeared in several collections, having been imported under the name of *Eugene Beauharnais*, nor does the transmutation of names appear to have stopped there, for I have recently seen it travelling under the name of *Bourbon Beauharnais;* it grows freely, and is well worth cultivating. *Rubens*, or *Ruban Pourpre*, of the English, is a distinct rosy-violet coloured variety, with perfectly formed flowers, though not so strong in growth as many others. *Semper-florens;* this is the far famed crimson Chinese, or *Sanguinea Rose*, the type of all the scarlet or crimson varieties of this division; it is perfectly double, cup shaped, of a rich crimson colour, and is universally cultivated; its nature is not so hardy as some others, but yet it withstands our winters with very simple protection, and though of humble growth gives a profusion of bloom throughout the entire season. *Triomphant*, or *Bengal Triomphant*, is a popular rose, very large and full, of a violet-crimson colour, and may be often seen of every shade, from rosy-lilac to violet-crimson; the flowers are always perfect in form. The plant has passed under several other names in Europe, such as *La Superba, Grande et Belle, Pæony Noisette*,

&c., but is known with us under the two former names only. *Triomph de Gand* approaches the former, but the colours are not so varied, and the plant is more robust in habit. *Vinella* is a very old dark crimson rose, remarkable for its blooming perfectly, only when the weather is very hot; it stands erect, when many others fade under the oppressive sun of the months of July and August. *Washington*, was one of our first American seedling roses, grown by the old house of D. and C. Landreth; it is yet a distinct variety in both flowers and foliage; the former are crimson, with white at the bottom of the petals, and frequently striped much more distinctly than *Don Carlos;* the foliage is a pale peculiar green, with red nerves; it grows and blooms freely.

This tribe of the rose family is yet susceptible of great improvement; we want some of pale rose and blush colours, with a few of dark rich crimson. For the former, we strongly urge the impregnating of *Meillez* with *Bosanquet* and *Queen of Lombardy;* and *Roi des Cramoises* with *Marjolin;* the offspring of these will doubtless give some choice sorts. We have plants of one and two years growth from many of the finest Bengals, but they have not yet arrived to such perfection of growth and inflorescence as to enable us to decide upon their respective merits. It now requires a very

choice article to rank among first rate roses, and
none shall ever, with our consent, be sent forth with
a name, without merit. Standards, or rose trees
of from one to three feet of the Bengal sorts, are
very attractive, and should always be cultivated
where variety, character, and ornament are desired. They can be very easily budded on any of
the Boursaults, or varieties of the Prairie Rose; on
either of which they will grow freely for a few
years, and with care may continue to flourish from
ten to fifteen years, keeping their heads close
pruned, and giving them plenty of enriching ma-
terials about their roots every winter. Some of
the delicate growing varieties can be budded on
the stronger sorts; the common daily rose makes
an excellent stock, and it can be propagated with
such facility that any quantity of strong plants
may be got for the purpose. All the China roses
can be propagated by cuttings taken from the
plants as soon as they have done blooming, in
June or August; the shoots, about three or four
inches long, that have produced flowers, are the
best for the purpose; cut them off close to the old
wood, and reduce them to three inches in length,
cutting off the top; then insert them into sandy
rich earth, in a shady spot, or on the north side of
a fence, or in a frame where they can be shaded
from the sun; it is necessary to make the cuttings

firm in the soil, leaving about an inch of the top
above ground, with one or two leaves thereon; give
them a sprinkling of water every evening for a few
weeks, when they will be rooted, and may then be left
to take their chance; if put in in June they will form
strong plants before winter; but where they are only
required to a limited extent, layering will be found
the safest method, and will always produce a good
strong plant.   For this purpose, select a shoot in
August, about a foot long; cut and place it into
the ground as directed for layering in a former part
of this work.   When fully rooted, about the end of
October, they can be cut off and put away into
winter quarters, either by the heels in a frame, or
planted into pots.   They must be shaded from the
sun for a few days after removal, and will be
greatly strengthened by having their tops cut off,
only leaving one, or at most two, branches, six to
eight inches long.   Those of robust habit do not
make handsome standards; they shoot away into
irregular forms, and require to be repeatedly trim-
med into shape during the growing season.   Summer pruning has been strongly urged upon the horticulturist by many writers in Europe, where they
have a cool humid climate to operate in; but in
this country, where growth is so rapid, it requires
all the foliage a plant produces to convey to the
roots the nourishment (carbonic acid) it derives

from the atmosphere, to support their free growth during the months of July and August. Every leaf, young shoot, or branch that a tree or plant is deprived of, during the period of their growth, is merely withdrawing from them a portion of their daily food. I have rarely seen summer pruning attended with beneficial results, but the contrary. The proper method is to disbud, or merely take the *tip* from the extremity of a shoot. "The size of a plant is proportional to the surface of the organs which are destined to convey food to it. A plant gains another mouth and stomach with every new fibre of root and every new leaf." When the Bengal, or any of the Tea roses, that have been planted in the open ground during the summer, are wanted to decorate the green-house, or parlour, during the fall or winter months, the best plan is, towards the middle of September, to cut the roots round each plant, leaving the ball of ground less than the pot you intend using. Cutting the roots will cause the plant to droop, but in about a fortnight they will make fresh rootlets, and will be ready for potting, which must be done with care, not to crumble the ball of earth or disturb the fresh roots. By this means the plants will look more handsome than if they had been grown in pots.

12

ROSA LAWRENCIANA.

THE MINIATURE ROSE.

THESE diminutive roses, were first introduced from China, where the greatest efforts of horticulture are directed towards dwarfing every tree, shrub, or plant.   In this instance, however, it is no peculiar mode of treatment that has stunted the growth of the plant, or diminished the size of the flowers; but these roses have been the produce of seeds saved from the smallest flowers of the kind, year after year, till they now have become the fairies of the tribe.   In France they cultivate about a dozen varieties of these Lilliputians, varying in colour from nearly white to dark crimson.   In this country, where almost every flower must be a Goliah, before it is admired, this family has been nearly lost sight of.   Indeed, they are entirely buried, when planted among those gorgeous flowers we have already attempted faintly to describe. It is therefore necessary, in cultivating the miniature rose, to grow them in a spot by themselves; for this purpose a slightly elevated position is the best, the ground having been prepared in the same manner as directed for Bengals or Teas.   The following are the most distinct varieties of European origin. *La Miniature*, a bright pink rose, perfect in character, with the flower about the size of half a dime, the plant about six inches high when full grown. *Gloire*, crimson, in size and growth rather larger than the former. *Pompon*, of the French, is our old Indica Minor, from which no doubt they have originated. *Bijou* is a clear rose colour, very similar to the first named, but a few shades darker. There is also the *Pretty American*, a plant of low stature, never exceeding six or seven inches in height, grown by Mr. Boll, of New York. And last and least, we copy from the third volume of Hovey's Magazine of Horticulture an account of the Prince of Dwarfs, which originated at Mr. S. Feasts, of Baltimore.—" When three years old, the *Master Burke* had fine full blown and very double flowers; and the half of a common hen's egg-shell would have covered the whole bush without touching it. This I saw and assert to be a fact. It is now seven or eight years old, flowers regularly every year, affording wood for propagation, and has never yet attained two inches in height, nor its whole top exceeded one, or one and a half inch in diameter; the rose is about the size of a buckshot." The article was written by a gentleman of high standing, with whom I am personally ac-

quainted, and do suppose, as he says it is, "a fact,"
although I have not been able to get possession of
the plant.

ROSA BOURBONIANA.

THE BOURBON ROSE.

IT is about six years since we predicted that this
group of roses, in a few years, would be the most
popular of the whole family of the "Queen of
Flowers;" that prediction is now literally fulfilled,
in the great demand by all the admirers and cultivators of the rose, for the varieties of this family.
Our readers will allow that the taste thus created
within a few years is not to be wondered at, when
we have held up to their admiration the choice
bouquet of these flowers which we have now to
present. As this family has become so very popular, its history, no doubt, will prove interesting to
many, and is indeed worthy of some attention.

The first of this rose is said to have been imported from the Isle of Bourbon to France in 1822,
and is there known in the catalogue of the French
growers as *Rose de L'Ile de Bourbon.* It attracted

great attention by its peculiar habit and profusion of brilliant bright rose coloured flowers, blooming in June, with a slight tendency to flower again in autumn; not being fully double, it produced an abundance of seed, from which varieties were obtained that bloomed freely the whole season. The only roses known on the island, were the common China, and the Red-four-seasons, till about the year 1816, when a Monsieur Perichon was planting a hedge of these, and among his plants found one very different from the others in its shoots and leaves, which induced him to plant it in his garden, where it was discovered by a French botanist, and sent home in 1822 to Monsieur Jacques, then gardener at the Château de Neuilly; this accounts for the name of "Bourbon Jacques," frequently given by English growers to the common Bourbon rose. It was introduced to this country, in 1828, by the late Mr. Thomas Hibbert, whose name will always be associated in the memory of many with rose culture. This association of ideas, connected with a particular subject, often flashes on the mind with the vividness of a sunbeam. The first perfect specimen I ever saw of this rose, was in the possession of that cultivator, and although it is now fourteen years ago, the spot, the company, the remarks, the very words, all recur to me most forcibly whenever this rose is introduced; "thus

12*

thought follows thought, according to the order in which objects and events are related to each other." The perpetuity of bloom, and the hardy nature of the Bourbon Rose fills up a chasm that had long been deplored by amateurs and cultivators in northern latitudes. They are decidedly more robust, and withstand a greater degree of cold than either the Noisette, Tea, or Bengal roses. It is now our impression, that in a few years, these, with the "Remontante" family, will be the only roses cultivated in all the states north of Virginia; and there is no reason why, in time, there should not be among them specimens exhibiting all the distinctive varieties disseminated among other groups, such as mossy, striped, spotted, mottled, not excepting a yellow colour in its brightest shade. In those now described, every colour will be found, from nearly pure white to dark crimson purple.

Acidalie, has been in cultivation several years, but is only now coming into notice for its distinct pale rose-white colour; the flower is perfect in form, large, and a little fragrant; the plant is quite hardy, and grows well. *Augustine Lelieur,* possesses considerable fragrance, is of a rosy-purple colour, full, round, well formed, and is a strong grower, but does not open well in the early part of the season. *Amourette,* is a pale flesh-coloured variety, with flowers very perfect and distinct; though smaller than many others it is very profuse. *Asteroide,* is of a bright rose colour, fully double, growing freely. *Bizarine,* is of the medium size, of a fine cup form, perfectly double; colour rosy-crimson, growth very strong. *Bouquet de Flore,* is a great favourite, and though it has been cultivated some years, is yet quite scarce; the flowers are very large, perfectly double, with large round firm petals, blooming very profusely; it possesses considerable fragrance, is a strong grower, and quite hardy. *Cardinal Fesch,* is the reverse in growth; the flowers are of a deep crimson colour, of medium size, but produced in profusion, quite double and distinct, and cannot be mistaken. *Célimene,* grows with vigour; the shoots are densely studded with strong prickles; flowers of a delicate rose colour, medium size, and fully double. *Ceres* is a rosy lilac, perfectly double, but does not open well in the early part of the season; it grows with rapidity, and opens fully after midsummer. *Docteur Roques,* or *Crimson Globe,* of the English, is of robust habit, makes an elegant standard; the flowers are globular, finely formed, of a rich dark crimson colour, the plant perfectly distinct, and when once seen it cannot be mistaken. *D' Yebles* grows very like the old Madam Desprez, but the flowers are of a much brighter colour, the foliage very large, and the plant quite strong. *Emilie Courtier*, does not appear to open freely till after July, when it shows its fine rose coloured fragrant flowers in great perfection. *Fédora*, is one of the new crimson varieties, perfectly double, a strong grower, and will yet prove to be a fine pillar rose. *General Dubourg*, when well grown, produces its large pale rose coloured flowers in great clusters, highly fragrant, giving a profuse autumnal blooming; it is a strong grower, and makes a fine pillar variety. *Gloire de Rosamène*, for profusion of bloom from June till severe frost, has not an equal; the flowers are nearly bright scarlet, produced in large clusters, but are not fully double, of rampant growth, making a fine pillar plant, very conspicuous in the distance, clothed with large foliage from bottom to top. *Grand Capitaine*, has produced quite an excitement among rose growers; very few plants of it ever having as yet come to this country, it has given an opportunity to some to supply the demand with other varieties under this denomination, not thinking, with the poet, that there was "nothing in a name." It is a bright crimson, perfectly double, globular form, foliage deeply serrated, wood of short firm growth, with few prickles. *Hennequin*, in growth, is much stronger than Madam Desprez, and very much of its habit, flowering in immense clusters of rosy crimson flowers. When on its own roots, in rich light ground, it will grow to any size. *Hermosa*, or *Armosa*, of some, has been cultivated these ten years, and is still a favourite; the flowers are of the most exquisite form, perfectly cupped; though under the medium size, the deficiency is made up in the profusion of pale rose coloured flowers. It is a dwarf grower, and makes a fine bush or standard; it also does well in the green-house. *Henry Plantier*, is a popular variety, producing a profusion of deep rose coloured flowers of medium size; it is a free grower, and will make a fine pillar variety. *Le Phenix*, is a bright red, with flowers beautifully imbricated to the very centre. Its habit is similar to Hermosa. *Madam Aude*, is a new bright rose coloured sort, with finely formed flowers; it grows vigorously, and will make a good pillar plant. *Madam Desprez;* it is eleven years since I first imported this rose, together with Aimée Vibert, Lamarque, Jaune Desprez, and some others of equal celebrity; they will maintain their character for a quarter of a century to come, and should be in every garden between this and Nachitoches. This rose originated with Monsieur Desprez, a distinguished French amateur; it is considerably hybridized with the Noisette, and like that rose produces its bright rose coloured flowers in immense clusters;

from thirty to seventy bloom in each when the plant is fully established; the foliage is a rich green, strong and handsome. *Madam Neumann, Le Brun, Gloire de France,* or the *Monthly Cabbage,* appear to be one and the same rose. I have repeatedly gone from plant to plant, and compared flower with flower, but could come to no other conclusion; when Le Brun appeared with so fine a character, about three years ago, I tried to persuade myself it was a *new* rose, but in vain; if they are not *one* and the same, they are at least perfectly similar, producing fine large deep rose coloured flowers of exquisite fragrance, but do not open well in the early part of the season, or during wet weather; they are of strong growth, requiring very rich soil. *Maréchal de Villars* is a very beautiful and distinct rose, with bright rosy-purple flowers, very compact, blooming profusely in either wet or dry soils; it is a good grower, and will always reward the care bestowed upon it; it will grow either as a bush or pillar rose. *Ninon de Lenclos,* is a free growing deep rosy purple variety, but never shows its character of free blooming till well established; whereas many Bourbon Roses bloom when a few inches high. *Paul Joseph,* is quite a new variety, and of course is to eclipse all its predecessors; the beauty of growth, symmetry of flower, brilliant crimson colour, rich large foli-

age, are all charms which it really possesses, and it
will some time enjoy its reputation, till another star
has the ascendant; every year brings with it some
particular plant possessing beauties that outshine
all others; thus we have had *Dr. Roques, Grand
Capitaine,* now *Paul Joseph,* next I suppose will
be the unequalled (as yet unseen) "Vicomtesse de
Reseguire," a large double pure white, edged with
rose. *Phillipar,* is a very distinct Bourbon, of a
beautiful peach-blossom colour; the plant grows
rapidly when well established, producing very
large clusters of flowers, rather under medium
size, but in profusion, forming a handsome pillar
plant. *Proserpine,* has more of purple in its
colour than any of the others; the flowers are
very perfectly formed; they have been small with
us, but no doubt will be much larger when once
the plant becomes established; it is yet quite new.
Reine des Iles de Bourbon, or the *Queen of the
Bourbons,* has been admired ever since it made its
appearance in the family; at first it was thought to
be a Bengal, the same as "Madam Bosanquet,"
which is also classed by some among the Bourbons. The colour is a beautiful waxy blush, with
petals perfectly formed, bold, and cup-shaped; a
half-blown rose from this plant is loveliness itself;
the plant is rather dwarf in habit, but in a proper
climate and genial soil, will grow as high as de-

sired. *Thérèse Margat*, or *Madam Margat*, approaches "Phœnix," though perhaps not so bright; the flowers are beautifully cupped, quite double, and fragrant; it is of medium growth. *Thérésita* is of a bright rose colour, perfectly double, very distinct from any other sort, in its bushy growth and profusion of bloom. *Triomphe de Plantier* is another of the habit of Madam Desprez; the flowers are much darker, being of a fine bright crimson colour, of the most perfect form, and produced in large clusters. *Victoire Argentée* is one of the very pale Bourbons, of cup form, opening of a very light rose colour, fading to a pale blush; it is quite fragrant, growing and blooming freely. *Violet de Belgique* is one of the most fragrant of the family, having all the agreeable odour of the Damask Rose; the flowers are of noble form, large, and perfectly double; it is of good growth, and will prove to be one of the greatest favourites of the group; it is yet quite scarce. *Zulema,* has much of the Noisette character and colour in its flowers, being a pale blush, produced in immense clusters of forty to seventy in each when the plant is thoroughly grown; the growth and foliage have all the appearance of the Bourbon, and it makes a very desirable variety.

There are several others in this most interesting family well deserving notice, and even very desirable where a full collection is grown, although it must be confessed that there exists, in this tribe, great confusion in regard to name, and there are many instances of the same article passing under different names in different collections. Some of these errors have originated in this country, unintentionally, I presume; others have been committed in France, in sending out the article not *true* to name. It must also be conceded that our English brethren have their full share in these practices; and with their host of *synonymes* (to give them no harsher name) completely blindfold us. Under their " Crimson Globe" we discovered our friend " Dr. Roques;" and under their crimson " Madam Desprez," or " Splendens," we think we see our " Hennequin;" at all events, it is not the rose cultivated in France under the name of " Splendens." I have repeatedly imported it, and it always proved to be the same, a very inferior variety, with bright pink flowers, not in the least deserving a name among the truly splendid ones of the present day. There are also some recent additions, only known by name, with whose colour and character we have yet to be acquainted. The Bourbons, generally, make fine standard plants, either on low or high stems; as they are nearly all of strong growth, and produce a constant succession of bloom the whole season, they require to be

13

highly nourished, either with rich soils, or copious
waterings with liquid manure. If on standards,
the tops of them will be benefited if protected as
advised for Tea and Bengal roses; or the whole
plant may be removed to a shaded situation,
where, after sheltering them, lay them in by the
heels, and cover them with boards; when spring
opens prune them close, and plant them where
desired, in fresh prepared soil. This removal is
even beneficial to them, for it is well known to all
growers that the Rose is improved by a change of
soil, unless it be in those deep alluvial soils that
have never been cultivated; in such, the roots run
yearly in quest of, and obtain, genial nourishment
for any length of time. But in the eastern and
northern states, it is absolutely necessary to lift the
plants that are budded, and place them under protection. Those grown on their own roots may be
well surrounded with dry leaves, which will pro-
tect them from the sudden changes of our winter
seasons in latitudes north of this; and even if
their tops be destroyed, they will push vigorously
from the roots, and produce their flowers in full
perfection. They should not be allowed to go to
seed; remove the flower stems as soon as they are
faded; it increases the reproduction of bloom.

REMONTANTES,

OR HYBRID PERPETUAL ROSE.

THIS is a new tribe, that has originated within a few years, between the Perpetual and Bourbon Roses, possessing the beauty and fragrance of the former with the growth and foliage of the latter; they produce an abundance of flowers from June to November; they open a field of pleasure to the northern grower and amateur, which had hitherto, been reserved only to the rose fanciers of more favoured climes. They are equally as hardy as the common garden rose; and by careful cultivation, good soil, frequent waterings in dry weather, depriving them of all faded flower-stems, they will show flowers the whole season till destroyed by frost. Their general habit is robust and vigorous to a remarkable degree; their flowers large, perfect, fragrant, and of almost every colour. We cannot give any idea of the beauty they may attain to in the southern states, where the soil is so genial to their culture, but they cannot fail to grow and flower to the satisfaction of the most fastidious taste. The varieties are yet limited, compared with many of the families we have described, but a few years will multiply them to a greater extent. We cannot fully depend upon the very flattering, if not extravagant, descriptions, of many roses emanating from growers in every country. The beauties of the child are most evident to the parent; so with the rose; though its charms are sweet to all, yet they are sweeter to him whose fostering hand has raised it from seed. To obtain a new variety meriting extra notice, in this improving age, is no paltry affair; and many, like "Queen Victoria," are named before their merit has been fully tested, and sent out to the floricultural world, as it were, on trial. But we will mention only such in which there will be no fear of disappointment. *Aubernon*, is an excellent bloomer, even to profusion, with perfect bright rosy carmine flowers. Of the same character is *Augustine Mouchelet*, though more on the violet colour; it is also a rampant grower. *Clémentine Duval* has much of the character of a Bourbon, even to its dwarfness; the flowers are quite perfect, of a bright pink colour. *Comte de Paris* has magnificent large rosy-purple flowers, perfect in form, with a delicate fragrance, blooming superbly through the fall months. *Docteur Max* is a new variety, not yet fully proven, but promises well, with flowers of a crimson-violet colour, large and perfect, growing freely. *De Neuilly* is more dwarf than the former; the flowers are of a beautiful clear rose, spotted with white, and highly fragrant; it is a very perfect and distinct variety. *Duc d'Aumale* is a pale crimson rose, a strong grower and free bloomer. *Duchesse de Sutherland* is not so constant a bloomer as some others, but for rapid growth it has few equals among the tribe, and its very double flesh coloured flowers are quite beautiful. *Edouard Jess* has been a favourite with us these two years, and is still admired for the beautiful flowers, of a bright red circled by a pale tint, delightfully fragrant. *Emma Dampiere*, and *Fidouline* are both quite new varieties, just introduced from France as very superior varieties, of a delicate rose colour. *Fulgorie* is a noble rose, of a rosy crimson colour, very large and perfect, producing its flowers in clusters like the old monthly cabbage, but always opening handsomely; the wood is very strong and thickly studded with prickles. *Lady Fordwick*, is truly superb, growing freely, and producing the whole season a profusion of large perfectly double flowers, of a rosy-pink colour, with the odour of the Damask Rose. *Louis Bonaparte*, has immense rosy-lilac flowers, fully double, always perfect, growing with great luxuriance, and makes a splendid plant. *Madam Laffay* has as yet no equal in the group; it stands unrivalled both in perfection of flower and fragrance; the growth and foliage are luxuriant; the

13*

flowers large, double, and exquisitely formed, of a rich rosy-crimson colour, with the delightful fragrance of the Cabbage Rose. It originated with Monsieur Laffay, a celebrated rose-grower near Paris, who dedicated it to his wife. *Marechal Soult* is another charming variety, of a bright rosy-purple colour, very double, imbricated, and fragrant. *Mistress Elliott's* charms consist in its distinctive rosy-lilac flowers, blooming freely and growing vigorously, contrasting well with *Prudence Roeser*, which has a portion of the Noisette character in its disposition to cluster; the flowers are a beautiful pink, perfectly formed; though not so large as some others, it is a beautiful distinct variety. *Prince Albert's* magnificent rich crimson flowers are very grand, being of the most perfect cup form, inclining to globular; it grows strongly, and is very fragrant; its only fault is in its not blooming so profusely in the fall as some of the others; for constant profusion *Rivers* has greatly the preference; for during the whole season it produces its extremely large flowers in clusters of brilliant crimson inclining to scarlet; it is very fragrant, and a great favourite, but quite scarce. These varieties, with two exceptions, have all flowered under our observation, and are great acquisitions to the lover of the rose. From these descriptions, it will be observed that this group is deficient in flowers of a

a pale or white colour, which, for the present, is
certainly a defect. However, this fault will not be
long attributed to them, for this year (1844) has
brought to hand, in perfect order, a host of names
with plants to suit; and another season will prove
their qualities; then, with the great facilities for
propagating, and the many hands applied to it, no
rose can be, for any length of time, a rarity about
Philadelphia. Among the recent sorts we may
name those that are most esteemed in France,
where they have all been grown. *Comte d'Eu,*
La Reine, Lady Alice Peel, Docteur Marjolin,
Reine de La Guillotiere, Sisley, Yoland d'Arra-
gon, Zelpha, with several others, all described as
being beautiful in colour, from blush to crimson-
violet, and in form very superior. But no doubt
there will be many discrepancies when tested by
an eye that gives merit precedence over rarity.

This very magnificent group of the rose family
cannot be too extensively cultivated; they are
nearly, without exception, free bloomers; but to
have them in full perfection they should be deprived of a great portion of their first blooming
buds, and have a few of their shoots cut back.
Indeed, the principal part of their first buds can
easily be dispensed with; for it is then the *rosy sea-*
son; the great aim of the fancier and cultivator is
to extend that season, which, with the above sacri-

fice, is at once accomplished.   These plants, whose luxuriance and immense flowers (perhaps the largest known) have been the result of hybridizing and exciting culture, deserve all the care that can be bestowed upon them.   Every encouragement must be given to promote the growth of the plant, which is best done in the winter season by composts and manures, or in the summer by rich waterings; these waterings should not be given oftener than once a week.   As these roses are yet quite scarce on their own roots, we have introduced a standard rose, at page 87, to show their beauty and the effect they have.   When trained in that way they are gems in the parterre—regular nosegays elevated to a convenient distance to enjoy all their beauty and fragrance.   When there are mossy, yellow, and striped roses in this family, rose culture will have approached its climax.

PERPETUAL DAMASK ROSES.

FOURTEEN years ago, this division of the Rose was known only to a very limited extent, not going beyond the old *Monthly Damask* and the *Portland*—the types of the group, which in that

short period have become so extensive and varied
in colour and character that the parentage of many
is difficult to point out. But unfortunately there
are those that pass for *perpetual*, which, with all
our art we cannot cause to produce even a second
blooming in the season, except by demolishing all
the buds they form in June to make them flower
in September. Many of them have another feature of obstinacy, and this is, that in rooting by
layers, they nearly all, take two years to form rootlets; we have, in consequence, either to graft or bud
them on other roses at any desired height. Several of them were brought into notice before the
famous Bourbon Roses, and were looked upon as
the *ne plus ultra* of the Rosary. The perfection
and beauty of many of their flowers cannot even
yet be outvied, and their stiffness of habit is not
unpleasant when properly placed. The best form
to grow them is on standards, from six inches to
four feet high. They are perfectly hardy in all
latitudes where the Damask Rose will grow. In
bleak situations, where the thermometer falls frequently below zero, the stems are greatly benefited
by a covering of straw or matting. The rods that
support standards should be put on the south side
of the plant; the strong sun is thereby warded off
the stem, which is beneficial, both in summer and
winter. What we have said in regard to the rich

culture required for Remontantes roses is equally applicable to the Perpetual.

Among the many, we have selected those that are most distinct, and such as have the greatest tendency to give a succession of bloom. One of the darkest is *Antinous,* whose deep purple-crimson roses remind us of some of our old Gallica roses; it is quite double, perfect, and fragrant. *Bernard,* or *Perpetual Pompone,* is a lovely pink rose, of exquisite form, all the petals being like so many beautiful shells neatly put together; it is very similar to Joséphine Antoinette, but they are distinct. *Billiard,* is larger than the former, and more of the rose colour, perfectly double, fragrant, and a profuse bloomer. *Claire du Chatelet,* is a new bright rose coloured variety, with very large perfect flowers, of very distinct habit, and a free grower. *D'Angers,* though an old variety, still retains its character of a constant bloomer, with large flowers of a pale rose colour. *Desdemona,* for its delicate colour, and exquisite fragrance, is worthy of culture, though its tendency to autumnal blooming merely, is discouraging. *Duc d'Enghien* proves very desirable, being distinct both in its pale fleshy colour, and in its character of growth, and a free bloomer. *Du Roi,* or *Lees Crimson;* it is about thirty years since this famous rose was grown from seed in the gardens of one of

the royal palaces near Paris, remaining comparatively obscure, and was considered a rare article in
England in 1831, where I first saw it growing,
carefully surrounded with rods to keep its admirers
at a distance. In 1832 or 3 I imported it as the gem
of the day, and it is still admitted to be the king of
Perpetuals, blooming profusely and perfectly from
June till Christmas; the colour is bright red, (not
crimson,) a perfectly formed flower, with all the fragrance of the Damask Rose, and without any extra
pruning never fails to bloom the whole season,—
richly deserving a place in every garden. *De
Trianon*, is a pretty dwarf, of a rose colour, a
profuse bloomer; when budded about one foot
high is quite a neat affair. *Ebène*, is just introduced to our notice as the darkest of the perpetuals, of a fine violet colour, " La plus foncée de
l'espèce," " The darkest of the kind ;" another season will show us its true character. *Feburier*, has
brilliant flowers, perfectly formed, quite double; a
strong growing variety, and will apparently succeed
in any soil. *Isaure Lablée*, gives a beautiful succession of perfectly delicate pink flowers, very fragrant. *Jeanne Hachette*, if not the most constant,
is the largest rose of the group; I have measured it
six inches in diameter, very double, fragrant, of a
pale rose colour, and is a strong grower. *Jenny
Audio* does well on its own roots, making a perfect

dwarf, with very large flowers of a dark rose colour; but when budded it grows much stronger. The favourite *Joséphine Antoinette*, is a free bloomer, with flowers of the most perfect form, of a rosy pink colour, and delighfully fragrant. *Lady Seymour*, is quite a new variety, occasionally spotted with blush, on a bright rose ground; quite fragrant, and of perfect form. *La Gracieuse*, or *Volumineuse*, is very distinctive in flower and growth; is quite thorny, and grows freely; the flowers are perfectly double, of a pale rose colour. *La Mienne*, or *Gloire des Perpetuelles*, is a free bloomer throughout the season, with bright red flowers, of exquisite form, and very sweet scented. *La Reine*, or *Queen of Perpetuals*, deserves its name; its flowers open freely, of a pale rose colour, blooming freely all the season, holding its place with *Du Roi* in every character. *Lodoiska Marin*, has been long esteemed for its profusion of large pale flowers, blooming freely, quite double, and in clusters, showing well in the distance. *Mon-strueuse*, or *Grande Belle*, at first sight would be taken for *Jeanne Hatchette*, but it is darker in colour, neither is it so large as that variety; it is also a strong grower, and will train into any form as a standard. *Noël*, is a very pale pink, approaching blush, growing freely, and is a prolific variety, large and double. *Palmire*, or *Blush Perpetual*, is still esteemed as a free bloomer, and the colour is very desirable in this class, which is very deficient in light colours. *Portland Blanc*, however, is nearly white, a rose of large size, perfect in form, quite fragrant, and a good grower; it is yet scarce, but a few seasons will make it nearly as plentiful as any other variety. *Préval*, is of a pale flesh colour, cup shaped, very perfect, a profuse bloomer, fragrant, and highly esteemed. *Prud-homme*, has been always a favourite for its brilliancy and fragrance, giving a succession of flowers of perfect form. *Pulchérie*, is one of the darkest varieties in the group, being only a shade lighter than *Antinous*, and more perfect than that variety; the wood is very spiny, and when not in bloom would be taken for *Ferox*, a very distinct variety, with large flowers, of a light pink colour. I may also mention *Panaché de Girardon*, not for its beautifully striped character, but to speak of its self-coloured imperfect rosy-red flowers, called *Striped Perpetual;* I have grown it five years, and only once saw it have any pretensions to that distinction, and then it was more like a flower that had been exposed to a few drops of rain, than one naturally variegated; no good Striped Perpetual Rose has yet appeared. *Quatre Saisons*, or *Monthly Damask*, has been long an inhabitant of our gardens, where, when well established, and well nourished, it gives a great pro-

14

fusion of its delicate pink flowers, in clusters, the whole season; its fragrance, also, is so agreeable, that it makes it a great favourite with all. The *Quatre Saisons Blanc*, or *White Monthly Damask*, is not so constant a bloomer as the former, rarely putting forth a succession of flowers, unless in very rich light soil; it is very like the *White Damask*, which is often substituted for it, though it does not produce its bloom in close clusters, like the White Monthly. The *Perpetual White Moss* has already been noticed, but we may here say that it is a " Sport," as florists term it, from the White or Pink Monthly Damask; plants of it having been known to assume the habit of those varieties. *Rèquien*, is a very distinct rose, the flowers expanding large and flat, very double, of a pale flesh colour, with very strong foliage and habit. *Scotch Perpetual*, does not bloom so constantly as we might expect from the name; yet it gives occasional clusters of flowers of nearly a white colour, during the summer months; its foliage, too, is very distinct from any of those named; it has more of the brier character, and is very similar in growth to the old Scotch Rose. *Stanwell*, is an English variety; a true Perpetual, blooming profusely and constantly the whole summer, till late in the season. Its habit is also like a Scotch Rose, though stronger in all its parts, with large double pale blush flowers of exquisite fragrance. *Triomphe de Montmorency,* is a beautiful pink cupped flower, quite double, very fragrant, and an excellent variety.

It will be observed that this family, like the Bourbons and Remontantes, is very destitute of white flowers; nor is there a genuine striped variety among either, so that the hybridizer and amateur have yet a large and new field open to their operations. We would suggest that *Du Roi* and the White Monthly Damask be fertilized; the former seeds abundantly, and with the culture we have recommended, the seedlings will bloom in three years. Some have advanced that the finest roses from seed are always the longest in flowering; when there is any tardiness observed, a few buds can be put into stocks, which will hasten their inflorescence.

~~~~~~~~~~~~~~~~~~~~~~~~~~~~~~~~

ROSA MICROPHYLLA,

OR SMALL LEAVED ROSE.

THERE is nothing in the whole family that we have been engaged upon, so distinctive in flower and character as this group. The plants of the true Microphylla Rose are very beautiful; when in foliage, their small pinnated leaves are so unlike any other plant (except perhaps a Locust tree in miniature) that they are both interesting and agreeable. It has been known twenty years in Europe, having been brought from China, and supposed by some to have originated in that country from the old *Macartney* Rose. I consider it, however, a distinct species, in every particular, and this can be proven by any of my readers who may be fortunate enough to save seed from it. The produce (if not intermixed with others) will be pure Microphylla roses, retaining the character of foliage, spiny calyx, with single, half double, and perfectly double flowers, nearly all of a dark rose colour. The first of this rose, as we believe, was imported by us in 1830, and it is now extensively cultivated in every section of the country. Recent importations, denominated *Microphylla*, can barely be recognized as such; the popularity of the old variety has given circulation to many of the inferior *new* ones, which, after having been seen in bloom, are frequently thrown aside as worthless. They are generally hardy, in dry soils giving a succession of flowers throughout the season. They are adapted for training against fences, or low outbuildings, or they may be formed into handsome bushes of any shape; but a hedge of them is the *beau idéal* of the flower garden, which all may enjoy in any latitude south of this. The following sorts are worthy of all requisite culture, and will grow freely in any rich soil, avoiding low wet situations. *Carnea,* or *Rosea,* is the old variety known as the *Microphylla Rose;* its character is unique, with small neat dark green foliage. The flowers are large and very double, of a rose colour, produced at the extremity of the young shoots, in twos or threes, according to the strength of the plant; the calyx (the green cup round the base of the flower) is thick and prickly; hence it is called the "Burr Rose." *Coccinea,* and the beautiful dark variety *Rubra,* are in every particular the same, except the latter being darker in colour. *Rubra Variegata,* does not merit the variegated distinction; the circumference of the flower is merely shaded. These all have the peculiar prickly flower bud. *Purpurea,* is of a purple-crimson colour, very large, with the growth and habit of all the former, except the calyx being destitute of the prickles so characteristic in the others. *Violacea,* has also a smooth calyx; the flowers of a violet-purple colour, quite double. The plant is of upright growth, and quite luxuriant. The following varieties are all hybridized with other sorts, and do not form handsome plants for bushes or standards, but are well adapted for training to

14*

poles, columns, or trellising. *Alba Odorata*, or
the *Double White Microphylla*, grows very luxuriantly, frequently making shoots eight or ten feet
long in one season; and in warm soils, where the
season extends from March to December, they will
no doubt grow twenty feet. The flowers are very
large and double, of a yellowish-white, very fragrant, and look beautiful among the dark green
foliage. *Hybrida*, is also a strong grower, with
double flowers of a rosy-purple colour. *Luxembourg*, appears to be a hybrid from some of the
Noisettes, of whose character it greatly partakes;
the flowers are in clusters of a dull purple, very
double, and a little fragrant. *Maria Leonide* has
much of the *Macartney Rose* habit; the foliage
nearly round, quite dark green and shining, with a
tinge of red on the young wood; the flowers are
sweet scented, of a creamy-white colour, with a
delicate blush centre. There are several others
classed among these, which, as far as known to us,
are either entirely worthless, or are so like those
described, that it is questioned if they are not the
same; this is not surprising, for we have grown
many of them from seeds, and all were either
entirely single, or so much like the parent, that
they could not be distinguished from it; with the
exception of Rubra and Purpurea, which have
originated with us. A pure white, bright scarlet,

yellow, or striped variety, would be a great acquisition. We would therefore urge upon cultivators
and amateurs the propriety of sowing every seed,
never despairing of the results, till the object is
accomplished. Lovers of the rose in the more
northern states will find this family entirely too
tender for out-door culture, unless surrounded with
a quantity of dry leaves. They will not prosper if
lifted every year from the ground and put away, as
directed for Tea and Bengal roses; but where a
green-house, or even dry cellarage, is accessible,
they will grow magnificently in large pots and
tubs, making a superb ornamental plant for placing
in summer in any conspicuous situation.

ROSA MOSCHATA.

THE MUSK SCENTED ROSE.

THE *Musk Cluster* rose is an old inhabitant of
our gardens. Botanists consider it a distinct species,
and have named it from the peculiar and agreeable
odour it exhales in the evening, and in the cool
autumnal months, which is the season that it
flowers most abundantly, in large clusters, of a
yellowish-white colour. There are single, semi-

double, and fully double varieties of it; the latter
is the variety generally cultivated. It is a native
of India, from whence it was introduced. From
the seed of this plant the grand family of the Noisettes originated; though it is more delicate than
the generality of those plants, yet the same system
of treatment recommended for them may be adopted
with the Musk Clusters. We have had several
roses introduced to our notice, under the head of
Musk Scented, but they have nearly all proved
worthless,—mere "cumberers of the ground."
However, a few deserve a passing remark before
we close our descriptions of the rose. *Pink Musk
Cluster*, has flowers of a pale pink colour, quite
double, though the petals are rather loose; the
plant grows very strong, and partakes greatly of
the Noisettes. *Princesse de Nassau*, is a pure
Musk Rose, of a yellowish-white colour, very
double, though not so profuse as some others.
Ranunculus Musk Cluster, is a pure white, perfectly double; so very much so, that it does not
open well in moist weather; the musky odour is
not so strong in this as in the old variety. They
do well to be trained to pillars, fences, or trellises.
In the eastern states they must be well protected
in the winter season, covering their roots with a
quantity of dry leaves. They delight in dry situations and rich soil. There is great room for im-

provement in this group, and we call the attention of cultivators and amateurs to it, that they may yet bring to view flowers of more perfect character and of more brilliant colours than any of the preceding, and even possessing, in a greater degree, the odour which appertains to the original species. It is true we have the *Pink Musk Cluster, Red Musk Cluster, Frazerii,* and some others, but as we have already said, they are worthless.

CULTIVATION OF ROSES IN POTS.

FOR THE GREENHOUSE OR ROOMS.

A SELECTION, for this purpose, should be made from the Tea, Bengal, and Bourbon families, all on their own roots, or budded very low. Presuming that these roses are already in pots, or to be procured from the Nurserymen in the small* pot they are generally grown in for sale, they should at once be placed into those of six inches in diameter, carefully and freely watered, during

---

* The plants for winter blooming should be ordered from the venders of an extra size; the very small plants sold at *low* prices would defeat the object.

July and August, cutting off all the flower buds
they show in the latter month. About the middle
of September, shorten the overgrown shoots, and
thin out the slender ones, turn the plants out of the
pots, depriving them of some of the soil, and repot
in those of seven inches diameter, using a compost
of sand, turfy loam, and manure in equal proportions; they will also grow admirably in the black
soil, from the woods, composed principally of decayed leaves; put several pieces of broken crockery
in the bottom of the pot, then a portion of soil;
place the plant so that its surface roots should be
under the rim of the pot, and then fill all round
with the soil; put them in a situation partially
shaded,—water sparingly, till they begin to grow—
then expose them fully to the sun and water freely
every day.   There they may remain till the middle
or end of October, and in the South till November,
when they should be removed to the greenhouse
or rooms, for flowering. Previous to their removal,
the pots should be washed, and the plants neatly
tied up. Thus treated they will mature all the
buds they will then show, and produce a profusion
of flowers again in January and February. Where
there is the convenience of charcoal, it will be found
of prime utility in rose pot-culture, broken to the
size of nuts and about one-fifth mixed with the
soil; the roots will delight to ramble through it,

and the foliage will be of a richer and darker green; the surface of the soil must have frequent stirrings. The plants must be carefully examined, and when-ever infested by the aphis, or green-fly, they should be destroyed, if in the greenhouse, by tobacco smoke. But, if in rooms, that method cannot be well adopted, for the odour would penetrate into every part of the dwelling. They should in that case be brushed off into a pail of water; or the safest plan will be to make a strong tea of tobacco, fill a pail with it, and while in a tepid state invert the plant therein, holding the hand or a cloth over the surface of the pot to prevent the earth from tumbling out. Roses in pots are wonderfully bene-fited by a watering of manure water about once in two weeks. This water is very easily prepared either in town or country. The droppings from the horse or cow stable put into a large tub or barrel, with water kept over it for a week or two, occasionally stirred up; the water then poured or drawn off for use about the colour of good tea; or one quart of POUDRETTE, put into three gallons of water—stir it a few times,—in two days it will be fit for use. A new species of manure from the Islands of the Pacific, called GUANO, the deposit of sea-fowls that has accumulated for centuries, is very valuable for making liquid manure. A quarter of a pound, in three gallons of water, frequently stirred before using, will be found very nourishing; indeed one pound to sixteen gallons, will be strong enough to use by the inexperienced, for if used much stronger than I have stated, it would injure plants in pot culture. When required for the open ground, watering with any of these liquids may be made stronger, or used more frequently.

INSECTS INJURIOUS TO THE ROSE.

THERE are several very destructive, and in some seasons their depredations almost overpower the operator. In the eastern states, the *Slug* nearly destroys every leaf. A remedy against its ravages, brought into notice by Mr. Haggerston, gardener to J. P. Cushing, Esq., is to take two pounds of whale oil soap, dissolved in fifteen gallons of water, and to syringe the plants therewith in the evenings till the insects are destroyed. The plants must also be syringed with clean water in the mornings, or the cure would be almost as destructive and offensive as the disease. After the plants are clean, stir up the soil to refresh it from the effects of the waterings. *Green-fly* is easily destroyed by tobacco water, applied with the syringe in the evening, and again with pure water in the morning. This insect is most troublesome in city gardens, where the birds cannot feed upon it. The *Rose Bug* is another very destructive enemy, which can only be kept under by hand-picking; they are found upon the flowers as soon as open. There is also the *worm* that destroys the bud before it opens. We seldom observe this in the country, but in some seasons it abounds in the city or town gardens, and must be extirpated by the hand.

There is yet another; a fly in the early part of June, deposits its egg near the surface of the ground, into a strong young shoot, and is not discovered till July or August, when we see its effects from the dropping of the top of the young shoot. As soon as this is noticed, cut off about twelve inches of it, and the little grub will be found in its centre, which if allowed to remain will come out under a leaf, near the top, drop into the ground and live again to renew its depredations the following season.

MILDEW ON THE ROSE.

Under artificial culture, this disease is frequently observed; or, as some writers term it the effects of

15

the disease, very few agree as to its origin or character.   From our observation it appears to be
most common, where extremes of temperature pre-
vail; even in the open air this is plainly seen; in
July or August, we occasionally have a few cold
nights, succeeded by rain and warm weather, and
as certainly as that kind of weather occurs, as certainly does the mildew follow.   It is rarely seen in
our collection of roses, few of which are kept in
high temperatures, and when it appears, a few
syringes of sulphur water are applied, which destroys it.   We prepare sulphur water, by placing
in a small barrel a piece of unslacked lime, about
the size of a double fist, with five or six pounds of
flowers of sulphur, on which we pour a few gallons
of boiling water, covering it up for an hour, when
we stir it, till the whole of the sulphur has fallen to
the bottom.   After settling, we pour off the water
for use, putting about a quart of it to the gallon for
syringing.   A recent writer says, he uses one ounce
of nitre to one gallon of water, with which he
syringes the plants once in ten days, and finds it an
effectual cure.

PROPAGATION OF ROSES

THAT BLOOM THE WHOLE SEASON.

THESE may be propagated by budding, grafting, or layering, as directed for roses that bloom in June; as we have before said, the latter method is preferable, and makes very permanent plants. They are also extensively propagated by cuttings, which is the plan that now calls for our special notice. There are two periods of the season, June and September, in which this mode can be adopted extensively and successfully, with the families of Bengal, Tea, Noisette, Bourbon, and Remontantes, Roses; (Perpetual succeed best by budding.) In May or June, as soon as the young shoots have shed their first flowers they will be in a proper state for use. The cuttings may be made from two to four inches long, having at least three joints or buds, from the lower end of which cut off the leaf and smooth the bottom end, with a sharp knife, directly under an eye, leaving the other leaves un-touched; the cuttings may then be inserted about one and a half or two inches into very sandy soil, either in pots or in the ground; if in a frame, so much the better. Shade them from the sun during the day, and give them gentle sprinklings of water. They must also be protected from· heavy drying winds, and fully exposed to the dews of the night, which are very genial to them. In about three or four weeks they will be rooted, and may either remain where planted till autumn, or be at once transplanted into pots, and placed in the shade till they have taken fresh root. These cuttings will make fine plants for the next season, and by extra culture may be made fine plants for blooming in the green-house during winter. Cuttings taken off in September, and planted in a very settled situation, will be well rooted in the following spring, and may then be transplanted into any part of the garden. The latter period will be the best for all the southern states, and the former for the eastern states. Indeed, cuttings can be taken off and may be propagated successfully, at any period of the season, when the plant has just ceased to bloom, which is the grand criterion for propagating the rose. In some soils, of a close sandy nature, all that is required is merely to put in a small piece of a shoot, in moist cloudy weather, where it is shaded from the direct rays of the sun, and it will root in a few weeks without any other care.

Where there is the convenience of a forcing house, or hotbeds of manure, there is another period of the season when the rose may be extensively propagated, which is practised to a very great extent by nurserymen who commence forcing roses in February. As soon as they show bloom the shoots are cut into cuttings of two eyes each, and planted into very small pots, of very sandy soil; these are placed into a close warm hothouse, or hotbed, in a moist temperature of 70° to 80°, where they will root in from two to three weeks, and are frequently sold within six weeks from the time they were planted. The very scientific have resorted to another mode of multiplying, which, with many sorts, make strong plants in a very short time. They take the roots of common roses, that are about the size of a small quill, and cut them into lengths of two or three inches, whereon they graft a single eye from the young wood, (by the method of whip grafting,) plant them into pots, which they place into a close hotbed or house, as above stated, where they grow instantly, frequently making a fresh growth within two weeks from the time of planting. Single eyes are also planted up to the base of the leaf, partially covering the eye, in pots of fine sand, subjecting them to the same hotbed treatment; these also root freely, but take some time before they make strong plants. When these tender cuttings are made they must be carefully shaded from the sun, and must be sprinkled with tepid water every evening. When they have made a fresh growth they should be removed to another frame or house, with gentle heat, and have air every day to harden them; in a week or two they will be fit for larger pots, to grow therein all the summer, or planted into the open ground in May.

Amidst the lovely creation of the floral world, none combines so many attractions as the Rose, and we hope that our simple remarks on its propagation will enable all, who desire it, to increase any part of the family they happen to possess. If tried once, and successfully, the experiment will, no doubt, be renewed, and an innocent pride indulged in increasing the power of ministering to one's own taste, or of gratifying that of a friend. Many suffer a latent predilection for these fascinating pursuits to die away, from the idea of not possessing the skill requisite for cultivating plants; others think of the expense they would be led into on an unwarrantable indulgence. If the more fortunate or more skilful amateur knows of such person, he will greatly promote both their mental and bodily welfare, by presenting them with a few plants of the easiest culture, to prove to them how easy it is, not only to nurture, but to multiply their sources of pleasure, as healthful as it is innocent. If any of our readers have a spark of this taste within them, we say cherish it as you would cherish a *friend*. To the ladies especially, a love of floriculture brings with it, in every period of life, a train of pure enjoyments. Whilst the city belle blushes her delight at the sight of the magnificent bouquet destined to grace her fair hand in the haunts of pleasure—the face of the country maiden glows with still purer satisfaction as she presents to a parent the rose which her own care has brought to perfection. And the mother!—how many lessons of wisdom can she impart to her children whilst instilling into their young minds the love of this healthful pursuit, and teaching them to look up from the wonders spread around them, to Him who gave the rose its hue. To the time-stricken matron also, even after age has deprived her of the active enjoyments of this taste, many pleasures still remain; under the shade of some far spreading tree she can, from her rustic seat, enjoy the sight of well planned arrangements, executed under her own superintendence, or surrounded by some favourite plants, inhale the fragrance which comes to her blended with sweet recollections of the pleasing toils which ensured their present luxuriance. But it is to those who have known sorrow and affliction (and who has not?) that the love of flowers and gardening comes like a boon from heaven, to shed its soothing influence upon the heart. In showering upon this earth such profusion of blossoms of every odour,

God has permitted us to bask, as it were, in his visible smiles, and every Christian will love him better for loving the glowing proof of that goodness which disdains not to minister to every innocent pleasure of his creature man. We feel we have perhaps digressed too far, but every lover of horticulture will understand how we have been led away; and to others we can only repeat, "Try to love flowers—learn to cultivate them;— it will make you happier, it will make you better."

INDEX.

THE END.

THE

FARMER'S ENCYCLOPÆDIA,

AND DICTIONARY OF RURAL AFFAIRS,

EMBRACING ALL THE RECENT DISCOVERIES IN AGRICULTURAL
CHEMISTRY, ADAPTED TO THE COMPREHENSION OF
UNSCIENTIFIC READERS:

BY CUTHBERT W. JOHNSON.

Enlarged, Improved and adapted to the United States,

BY A PRACTICAL FARMER,

ASSISTED BY NUMEROUS SCIENTIFIC GENTLEMEN.

This invaluable work is now completed in one splendid Royal
Octavo Volume, of upwards of 1150 closely printed pages,

WITH SEVENTEEN BEAUTIFULLY EXECUTED PLATES

of Cattle, Agricultural Implements, Varieties of Grasses, Destructive Insects, etc.

And Numerous Woodcuts.

Price, well bound in leather, only FOUR DOLLARS.

The work upon husbandry now ushered before the American public is the production of an English gentleman of great intelligence, assisted by some of the best authorities upon rural subjects in his country. By collecting and condensing the most interesting details relative to farming, chiefly derived from living authors, such as Professors LIEBIG, LOWE, Sir J. E. SMITH, BRANDE, YOUATT, STEPHENS, THOMPSON, LINDLEY, I F JOHNSON. etc. etc., he has been enabled to present the very latest information, and furnish a fund of matter which cannot fail to attract all who take an interest in rural affairs, so long studied, and so thoroughly understood as these must needs be in Great Britain.

The absence of speculative views, with the very practical and matter-of-fact character of the information given upon all subjects treated of, will per-haps be found to constitute the highest recommendation of "Johnson's Farm-er's Encyclopædia, and Dictionary of Rural Affairs."

"No farmer or planter who desires to be master of the science of his pro-fession should be without this work."—*Am. Farmer.*

"An excellent manual of agriculture—and we venture to say that there is not a farmer in the United States that cannot derive many useful hints and much valuable information from this Encyclopædia."—*The Cultivator.*

"Should be in the library of every farmer."—*American Agr.*

"We heartily recommend it to our readers, and wish every farmer in North Carolina would take it and study it carefully."—*Raleigh Star.*

"We have now received twelve numbers of this truly valuable work, and have examined them thoroughly. Its merits are far greater than we had be-fore imagined, and we are fully convinced that such an amount of valuable knowledge for farmers can be found in no other work in so cheap and con-venient a form. In fact, no farmer who pretends to be well informed in his profession should consent to be without it. As a book of reference, it is in-valuable—we would not be without it for four times its cost."—*New Genesee Farmer.*